709.22

BU 24/11/17.
EA 30/5/17
NE 3/10/17
M 6-2-18
BU 12/6/18

Zag 20/11/18

MC Box 02/19
Tu 26/7/19
Su 30/4/19

EA 30/9/20

M 27-9-16

Return this item by the last date shown.
Items may be renewed by telephone or at
www.ercultureandleisure.org/libraries

east renfrewshire
CULTURE
and LEISURE

Barrhead	0141 577 3518	Mearns	0141 577 4979
Busby	0141 577 4971	Neilston	0141 577 4981
Clarkston	0141 577 4972	Netherlee	0141 637 5102
Eaglesham	0141 577 3932	Thornliebank	0141 577 4983
Giffnock	0141 577 4976	Uplawmoor	01505 850564

Alexandra Connor was born in Lancashire and educated in Yorkshire. She has had a variety of careers, including photographic model, cinema manager, and personal assistant to a world-famous heart surgeon. Yet it was only after being stalked and assaulted in London that she found her real forte — during her convalescence, she discovered an ability to paint, and a further relapse resulted in the writing of her first novel. Although traumatic, Alexandra believes that the assault changed her, and gave her a life she could never have imagined before. She still has strong connections to Lancashire today; and as well as being a highly popular novelist, she is a presenter on television and BBC radio.

You can discover more about the author at www.alexandra-connor.co.uk

PRIVATE VIEW

Behind universally admired works of art — *The Laughing Cavalier* by Hals, *The Birth of Venus* by Botticelli, *The Thinker* by Rodin, and many more — are the artists themselves, whose lesser-known eccentricities are revealed in *Private View*. Here is Fra Filippo Lippi, a friar who had to be locked in a room by the Pope in order to keep him at the easel and away from the bedroom. William Blake, who talked to the dead — and Théodore Géricault, who brought the dead home with him to use as unpaid models. Here is Rembrandt, who not only owned a monkey himself, but once painted a similar creature into a patron's family portrait. And of course the swaggering Michelangelo, who as a child recommended his 'perfect' services 'in all humility' to the Duke of Milan . . .

Books by Alexandra Connor
Published by Ulverscroft:

THE MOON IS MY WITNESS
MIDNIGHT'S SMILING
THE SIXPENNY WINNER
THE FACE IN THE LOCKET
THE TURN OF THE TIDE
THE TAILOR'S WIFE
THE LYDGATE WIDOW
THE WATCHMAN'S DAUGHTER
THE SOLDIER'S WOMAN
THE WITCH MARK
MASK OF FORTUNE

ALEXANDRA CONNOR

PRIVATE VIEW

The Secret Lives of the
World's Great Artists

Complete and Unabridged

CHARNWOOD
Leicester

First published in Great Britain in 1989
under the title *The Wrong Side of the Canvas* by
Robson Books Limited
London

First Charnwood Edition
published 2016

*A catalogue record for this book is available
from the British Library.*

ISBN 978–1–4448–2956–3

Published by
F. A. Thorpe (Publishing)
Anstey, Leicestershire

Set by Words & Graphics Ltd.
Anstey, Leicestershire
Printed and bound in Great Britain by
T. J. International Ltd., Padstow, Cornwall

This book is printed on acid-free paper

This book is dedicated to my life-support machine. In other words, my mother, Honey.

Contents

Prologue

This book is dedicated to all the people who have been: (a) pressed up to the third button of a Viyella shirt at a crowded private showing as an 'expert' comments loudly on the paintings; or (b) have read or watched long-winded explanations from the latest artistic guru, who is determined that art should be taken very, very seriously.

Both species of experts are to be avoided at all costs.

This is a problem that has been endured for centuries. No doubt high-toned louts pontificated in the Senate, dressed in unique three-piece togas and peeling grapes as they tore apart the latest marble statue, hot from Rome. Certainly artistic oafs prowled the Victorian scene, categorizing artists with all the subtlety of a clay-pigeon shooter firing into thick fog. Titian was 'too red'; Rubens 'too fleshy'; and Turner was 'a madman with cataracts.' In the face of such criticism, lesser mortals bowed to the experts, and thus the reputation of a painter would be sold down the river with barely a backward glance.

But, worst of all, these types of people make art dull, boring, tedious, dry, dingy, and deadly. They talk about painters with hushed reverence, regarding each picture as something to be seriously studied, not enjoyed. But help is at hand! This book is designed to enable the art-lover to stun everyone with the astonishing range of his knowledge — knowledge that (dare I say it?) has found humor, among other things, in painting. Read on, and find sensations leaping off every page as you discover that Titian liked company (he was notorious for his orgies), that Caravaggio was a bad sport (he murdered his tennis partner), and that Frans Hals, of *The Laughing Cavalier* fame, brought his wife around to his way of thinking with the flat of his hand.

Contrary to what the boring academics tell you, murder, sex, and humor were the order of the day, as painters competed ferociously with one another. Art was then a *part* of everyone's life and the artists themselves became a part of the astonishing times in which they worked. Rivals murdered one another, shared lovers, stole from one another, and generally fought to survive in surroundings that were remarkable in themselves.

Thankfully, they were all human — in some cases, more human than was good for them. Knowing their faults doesn't make the artists any less great as painters, but it certainly helps us to know that they were less than perfect without a brush in their mitts. It's time they were dusted off and brought out into the daylight, where they can be enjoyed.

So if you want to be invited to every private showing to give a truly unique insight into any exhibition, if you want to silence pompous strutters with your knowledge of what the painter did (and to whom), keep turning the pages and increase your circle of friends and your dinner engagements as you discover another way of looking at art — from the wrong side of the canvas. Read on and, next time you're looking at Velázquez's *Las Meninas* and someone is pronouncing on the skill of the brushwork, simply lean forward and say, 'It's a shame about the poor sod with syphilis in the background, isn't it?'

1

The Artists' Lives

Under the all-embracing title of 'art,' people have long accepted behavior from painters that would, in other people, qualify them for a long stay in a safe place. In the early 1500s, for instance, because Michelangelo was working on the interior decor of the Sistine Chapel, the fact that his breeches had to be *cut* off him after six months qualified as a harmless eccentricity rather than a health risk. (Incidentally, when the trousers came off, so did some of his skin.)

Michelangelo was not the only artist with an aversion to water — fifty years or so later, Caravaggio bought fabulous clothes as soon as he had sold a painting, only to wear them until they fell apart. He also used one of his pictures as a tablecloth, and urinated in his paint to dilute it. (This in itself was not unique; others are known to have used feces as a thickening agent.)

The old adage of 'you are what you paint' is certainly true for Adriaen Brouwer. He was a dissolute rake who spent his time either painting debauched scenes in taverns or experiencing them. He liked women, drinking, women, singing, women, and general abuse, but he also had a weakness for politics. His political enthusiasm cost him his freedom and in 1631 led to his confinement in prison, where he languished, unhappily missing his life of women, drinking, and singing . . .

But dissipated as he was, Brouwer was no chump and, like most politicians, could turn every situation to his advantage. Even in jail, he could recognize an opportunity when he saw one, and although his painting was somewhat restricted, his ambition was not. There can't have been many artists who left prison with a pupil. But Brouwer did just that, apprenticing the jail baker, Joos van Craesbeck — a case of give us this day our daily bread?

Mind you, Brouwer had had a bad start. His mother, a seamstress, had decided that her prodigy should be apprenticed to a master painter to make full use of his talents. Unfortunately, the good woman chose Frans Hals to teach her son. For a long time, people have smiled at *The Laughing Cavalier* and decided that Hals must have been a fine fellow to have painted it — but he was actually a drunk, who worked off his temper on his wife, after squandering all the money he made. Perhaps the only thing that could be said in his favor was that he was consistent: not only the family suffered but his apprentices also, who were starved and overworked. In his eighties, Frans Hals had lost his position and his money, and ended his days in a poorhouse (ironically having painted the same place years earlier when he was prosperous).

Dissolution on a truly memorable scale was embraced by Modigliani in this century. This artist, whose elongated portraits are now commanding high-blood-pressure prices at auction, did not feel the need to dedicate himself to his art; instead, he swore early on, 'I am going to drink myself dead,' and took to the task with remarkable dedication. The added addictions of hard drugs and soft women soon hastened his entry into the next world, and he arrived, seriously raddled, at the Pearly Gates when he was only thirty-six.

But if Modigliani didn't care a damn about what people thought, Sir Joshua Reynolds did, a century and a half earlier. Reynolds was *very* serious about art, and very serious about the respect he thought due to the artist. He also had a stranglehold on the artistic world of the day and was admired and respected by the likes of Edmund Burke (the statesman and philosopher) and Dr. Johnson. Reynolds liked to keep grand company — bishops, intellectuals, actresses, and famous courtesans — but he also liked the taverns and the theater (although his enjoyment of the plays must have been somewhat curtailed by his poor hearing). London society was his to enjoy as he joined numerous clubs and rose to eminence, cultivating powerful friends, although the king, George III, remained irritatingly unimpressed.

The king preferred other painters, and it was only after the death of Allan Ramsay (the previous royal dauber) that Reynolds got his first whiff of regal patronage. After an exhausting delay, he was finally beckoned to court to be told that he was now the official 'Painter in Ordinary to the King' — an honor he relished until

Reynolds discovered that his salary was less than that of the king's rat catcher.

But Reynolds weathered the blow and continued to progress, painting pictures of the high and mighty in a variety of poses borrowed from the antique. Some of these were successful; others were not. Some whey-faced eighteenth-century duchesses didn't look altogether convincing as dusky Grecian heroines. Reynolds was also a little eccentric in his choice of props. A pet macaw, often pressed into service as an exotic sitter, was given the run of the house, a maid being given the responsibility for cleaning up after it. Apparently, she hated the bird; the bird returned the feeling, and waited for its revenge. It was one of Reynolds's pupils who provided the perfect opportunity when he painted the maid's portrait — the macaw indulged in its own artistic criticism, and shredded the painting to ribbons.

Other props caused problems, too. One of Reynolds's sitters wanted his portrait painted with his hat on his head. Reynolds insisted that the hat should be held in the hand; the sitter refused. Reynolds conceded, up to a point. The actual portrait was painted with one hat on the sitter's head — and another hat under his arm.

Rembrandt was another painter who had curious ideas about props. After sitting for a large family portrait, the patron was astonished to find a monkey included in the picture. The monkey, he said reasonably, had not been ordered. Indeed, there was no point including it in the painting, as the patron did not have a monkey in his family, and, in short, the monkey had to go. Rembrandt dug in his heels: No monkey, no painting. The Dutch merchant dug in his heels: If you keep the monkey, you know what you can do with the painting. Rembrandt held his ground — and ended up with a huge family portrait in the attic, complete with monkey.

Michelangelo's near-contemporary Botticelli had a sense of humor, too, although looking at his picture *The Birth of Venus*, you would not presume that its painter liked a belly laugh. But Botticelli loved a good joke, especially at someone else's expense. According to Vasari (probably the first and most famous artistic biographer), a weaver had the misfortune to set up shop next door to the painter, and was informed almost immediately that his noise was disturbing Botticelli's creative process. The weaver replied that he had to make a living; Botticelli thought otherwise. Rolling an enormous stone onto the roof of his studio (which was higher than the weaver's), he placed it so that any vibration or noise from the weaver's loom would send it plummeting through the man's roof. Due to this subtle act of persuasion, the weaver and his loom remained obligingly mute.

Botticelli was a complicated man, and although he was a painter of genius, he was terrible with money. Well paid by the Pope, he still managed to spend his salary immediately and was soon begging for loans. His love of practical jokes and his reckless spending were not his only shortcomings; he also became committed to religion, and gave up his painting to follow the ill-fated Savonarola. In fact, he even joined a religious sect, the 'piagnoni,' or the 'snivelers,' as they were known.

The sect lived up to its name, and as Botticelli grew older and poorer, he had good reason to snivel. Finally, when he was almost destitute, Lorenzo de' Medici (who had never been the victim of one of the artist's practical jokes) took pity on him and came to his aid. But the damage had been done and Botticelli's sense of humor and his desire to work had completely vanished. He died crippled, neurotic, and troubled at the age of sixty-five.

But although some artists become victims of their times, others try to take advantage of other people's success. Simone Cantarini was a superb example of this. As a gifted painter in the early seventeenth century, he reckoned that all he had to do to get to the top was to infiltrate his way into some major artist's studio. The artist he picked was Guido Reni. Creeping and cringing about, Cantarini flattered and cajoled his way into the master's good books and finally was accepted into his studio and set to work. Unfortunately, his true colors soon showed. Spiteful and malicious, he complained about the conditions, the work, the pay — in short, he griped so much that Reni soon began to regret his act of charity.

Not that Cantarini was selectively spiteful. He was spiteful about everything and everyone — so much so that his tongue was feared not only in

6

the studio 'but in the whole of Bologna,' as well. Understandably, Reni soon tired of him. On your bike, he said finally. And off Cantarini went.

Incredibly, this viper did not sink without trace; due to his talent, he did well as a portrait painter and was rising in the artistic ranks nicely when he hit a setback. Artistic temperament being what it is, some artists do have a tendency to overreact, and Cantarini was no exception. On beginning to paint a portrait of the Duke of Mantua, he was stumped when he couldn't get a likeness. Now, another person might have tried again, or given the duke back his deposit — but not Cantarini. With a theatrical flourish wasted on an empty studio, he swallowed poison and expired before the failed work.

Artistic temperament shouldn't be discouraged; otherwise, we would all sink into a mire of mediocrity. But there is a limit, and Lucas van Leyden, a Dutch painter born in 1494, almost overdid it. Precociously gifted, he was also larger than life, throwing banquets for lesser painters with all the aplomb of a farmer scattering seed to a brood of scrawny chickens — and when he had finished gloating, he traveled around the world like an exotic nomad. Even when he got around to painting, he was unique, preserving most of his energy by working in bed, dressed immaculately in yellow silk attire and sipping the finest wines.

Lucas van Leyden wasn't the only painter to cut a dashing figure; Jean Etienne Liotard was a bit of a snappy dresser, too. This Swiss artist went on the inevitable grand tour and ended up in Constantinople. Before long, he had gone native, adopting the Turkish dress and growing a beard. One can imagine the sensation he caused walking about eighteenth-century London in the equivalent of a long frock. However, sensing a good publicity gag, he retained his dress and wallowed in the notoriety it brought him, painting portraits Walpole suggested were 'too like to please.'

Apart from the adoption of Arabian dress by Liotard, the cult of Orientalism spread far and wide, influencing such artists as Delacroix, who in 1838 painted *The Fanatics of Tangiers*. These fanatics were the type of sitters often referred to as 'colorful'; indeed, their jumping, leaping, screeching, and general foaming at the mouth would seem to make for a memorable painting. They were also fond of hashish, which helped them to reach a religious ecstasy so intense that they could walk on hot coals, eat snakes, and dance on swords without noticing their injuries.

There must be some connection between Delacroix's love of the romantic and his own beginnings. It would seem almost certain that the artist's real father was the French statesman Talleyrand, because M. Charles Delacroix was, at the time of the painter's conception, recovering from an operation to remove a tumor that had precluded any sexual activity for some time. (In fact, possibly proving the point, when Charles Delacroix died, a book on impotence was found among his possessions.)

The painter's life began surrounded by gossip, and as Delacroix grew, Talleyrand made sure that his son was protected and that he received much patronage. Apparently, the artist was fairly remarkable in appearance, too; 'a wild, exotic, almost disquieting beauty,' a contemporary remarked, thus leaving for all time an image to coincide conveniently with Delacroix's Romantic paintings.

Not that it was all plain sailing, for despite Talleyrand's assistance, Delacroix seems to have drawn his own conclusions about dear old Dad. His sketch of the *Man with Six Heads* sums up this adept turncoat politician perfectly. Perhaps because of Delacroix's erratic beginnings, he lived life to the full and was certainly no snob; in fact, he seduced women of all classes, and had affairs with a series of models, chambermaids, and peasant girls before succumbing to the tubercular laryngitis that dogged him intermittently. He was obsessed by love: 'I am unhappy . . . I need love . . . my painting would be quite different if I was constantly stimulated by the sweet warmth of love . . . '

Yet because he insisted on being provocative, Delacroix's paintings were often viciously criticized, and two paintings, *The Death of Sardanapalus* and *Liberty Leading the People*, were physically attacked. Understandably choked, Delacroix turned his back on France and set off on his travels again, returning only when his all-absorbing need for love was provided by Jenny le Guillou, who looked after his health and encouraged him in his work, though Delacroix cheated on her with the likes of George Sand. He also developed a deep love for Chopin and was shattered when he died.

From the 1830s, Delacroix enjoyed tremendous official favor, and worked avidly, slaving all day and then going to the fashionable theaters at night, his love affairs more limited as his work increased and his libido decreased. As he grew older, he became more detached from life, the artist Odile Redon remarking, 'He walked through the dark streets of Paris alone, with his head bowed, treading the pavement like a cat.'

In the end, Delacroix, one of the greatest Romantic painters who ever lived, died as romantically as he had lived — his hand clasped by his ever-faithful Jenny.

Delacroix wasn't the only artist with a towering imagination. Alessandro Algardi, a successful seventeenth-century sculptor, apparently possessed an imagination and memory that were almost superhuman. This sculptor did not like to be distracted by sitters (even if he happened to be working on their portraits!) and developed a clairvoyant ability to chip out a likeness without the aggravation of dealing with the sitter.

Unfortunately, although his work and wealth increased vastly, so did his girth, and in later years Algardi found himself too fat to carve, his stomach reaching the marble before he did, his hands immobilized before a rogue belly. Wealthy and lazy, he admitted defeat and let his assistants do all the work, dying, resplendently obese, at the age of fifty-nine.

Such a fate could never have befallen William Powell Frith, a Victorian painter who was very careful of his appearance and his status. This painter was something of an artistic paparazzo, his chief claim to fame being his ability to record the important people of the time — including courtesans, painters, writers, and various titled heads — and he provided an insight into the lives of the rich and famous, knowing that enough cheap prints would sell to make *him* rich and famous, too. Employing a clever marketing ruse, he exhibited scenes of the fashionable Victorian haunts and, as expected, the public flocked to see them. His 1858 painting *Derby Day* is a perfect example. There is not an inch of canvas, other than the sky, that does not sport a body of some sort. In fact, if one member of the crowd had been plucked out, the whole lot would have collapsed like a set of dominoes. The painting was so popular when it was exhibited that railings were put up to hold back the crowds who came to see it at the Royal Academy.

Frith continued painting crowds, in pictures such as *The Railway Station* (a place so well attended that no one could have emerged without a couple of cracked ribs). His painting *The Marriage of Their Royal Highnesses the Prince of Wales and the Princess Alexandra of Denmark* was also a triumph, containing over a hundred portraits and taking two years to complete.

Not everyone was smitten with Frith. The aesthetic critic Ruskin was not too keen on the painter, and a ditty was composed that summed up their relationship nicely:

I ups and paints, hears no complaints

11

And sells before I'm dry,
'Till savage Ruskin sticks his tusk in,
And all is up with I.

Frith's overwhelming love of the famous included the likes of Lillie Langtry, who appears in the picture *The Private View of the Royal Academy* along with Oscar Wilde, who was causing quite a stir at the time by walking around London in velvet kneebreeches, a velvet beret, silk stockings, and bearing a lily in his hand — a way of dressing that would be guaranteed to excite attention anywhere. Frith loved society and its little idiosyncrasies — like the young blonde in *At Homburg* lighting up a cigarette. She does it with the same defiance that the sixteenth-century Dutch employed when tobacco had the reputation marijuana has now.

Such antics were considered wonderfully daring and fashionable — as was gambling. Frith loved to paint the rich who ended up not-so-rich in fabulous locations, their misery exciting not sympathy in the viewer but a belief that they were 'getting their comeuppance' — which was exactly what Frith wanted. History painting also intrigued him, although he ended up portraying the same kind of woman in different clothes — Nell Gwynne and Lillie Langtry are sisters under the skin, after all.

Yet for all his success in his lifetime, Frith's reputation has faded: his paintings now look too like press photographs, and the myriad faces are not quite as intriguing, now that they are no longer known.

As we have already seen with Delacroix, having a famous father certainly helps the novice to obtain a good footing on the artistic ladder. John Hoppner, an English portrait painter of the eighteenth century, was from his early years in the fortunate position of receiving royal assistance. In fact, George III granted him an allowance to train at the Royal Academy Schools. Suitably aided, Hoppner glided through his studies; he received royal portrait commissions at the advanced age of twenty-seven, became Portrait Painter to the Prince of Wales, and generally rose faster than a helium balloon — thus giving rise to the belief that he was, in fact, the king's son.

Other artists did not find the road such a smooth one, and it is worth remembering that some of the most famous have had very bumpy rides. Auguste Rodin, the French sculptor, achieved fame but did not find critical success for some time. In fact, his career reads like a tragedy in many respects:

1. His sculpture *The Age of Bronze* was so lifelike that a story went around that it was taken off a life cast, and was therefore a cheat.
2. The base of his Claude Lorraine monument was changed to appease the town council.
3. Another council refused to exhibit his *Burghers* — (not Casey Jones but the Burghers of Calais).
4. *The Thinker* was hacked up with a meat ax

13

wielded by a lunatic.

5. His *General Lynch* was blown up in a Chilean revolution. (The sculpture, that is, I'm not sure what happened to the original.)
6. His Victor Hugo monument was altered repeatedly and was never exhibited in the form in which it had been commissioned.
7. Another committee refused his Balzac monument.
8. And finally, Rodin died before his *Gates of Hell* was finished. Now own up — who *still* wants to be an artist?

At least Rodin took it all on the chin, whereas, for all intents and purposes, Paul Cézanne was a bit more timid. Bullied by an overbearing father, he was forced to study law at the university, and when he failed at that, he left for Paris to study art. Not surprisingly, due to Cézanne's obsession with murder, orgies, and autopsies, he was a resounding failure and fled back home, and back under his father's control.

With the dedication of a true artist, Cézanne threw his paintbrushes to one side and worked at his father's bank for a while, until, incensed by Dad's increasing dominance (he opened all his son's letters), Cézanne returned to Paris to try his luck again. Buoyed up with enthusiasm, he vowed he would paint pictures 'which will make the Institute blush with rage and despair.'

He was right. They blushed. They raged. They despaired — and they rejected every one of his paintings.

Because Cézanne was financially dependent on his father, he lived in a kind of straitjacketed control, which continued throughout his life. Even when he became involved with his mistress, Cézanne was so cowed by his *père* that he hid her in L'Estaque. He was good at hiding — especially when the army came looking for him to fight the Prussians.

But Cézanne must have been a clever coward, because he remained lily-livered and at liberty, residing with his mistress and baby son, Paul — whose existence was also hidden from Cézanne senior. In fact, the whole family was rapidly becoming invisible, when, as luck would have it, Cézanne senior died and left his son an inheritance.

Finally financially secure, Cézanne concentrated on his painting. He was a painstaking worker and left many things unfinished, scrapping Vollard's portrait after over a hundred sittings because the shirt wasn't right. (After a hundred sittings, one would have thought it would have been out of fashion.) For the rest of his life, he worked, and had the satisfaction of being hailed as a genius in his own lifetime (even though he couldn't paint shirts).

Yet as we have already seen, the artistic life does not bring out the best in some people — as Adam Elsheimer found out. This sixteenth-century German landscape painter was very well thought of, and although his was an easy triumph, it resulted in melancholia or, as we would put it, a bad case of the blues. Maybe this condition wasn't helped by his going to Rome and coming into contact with Caravaggio — an experience most people found trying. Whatever the cause, Elsheimer's depression became so bad that he was unable to work and his pupil, scenting an advantage, exploited him to such an extent that his master was imprisoned for debt.

This turn of events did little to cheer him up and Elsheimer slipped further and further into the slough of despondency, his work neglected. Even Rubens, the most kind of men, remarked after his death, 'I pray that God has forgiven Signore Adam his sin of sloth' (they didn't rate depression as serious then, just sinful) '[which] caused himself much misery . . . and reduced himself into despair.'

Then, with typical resourcefulness, Rubens sold Elsheimer's pictures to raise money for his widow (a lady who had had problems of her own after fleeing from a charge of heresy), to relieve her from the destitution in which her husband had left her.

★ ★ ★

There is a saying, 'Never work with children or animals,' and Giovanni Battista Rosso, the sixteenth-century Italian, should have taken note of it. Rosso was a Florentine painter who kept a large ape, which was apparently very handy around the house. According to Rosso's contemporary Vasari, the ape fell in love with one of Rosso's apprentices, who, when working on a friar's premises, used to suspend the obliging ape from a window to steal the grapes off the vine.

16

The friar, suitably aggrieved by the state of his crop, sat on guard and, when he saw the ape, lunged at it with a stick! The ape responded by ripping up the whole vine and then falling off the roof, onto the friar.

Now apparently, this ape had a long memory, and when Rosso was forced to shackle it with a weight, the ape reasoned that it was the friar's fault and found its way onto the roof over the friar's room and crashed the weight up and down until all the tiles were broken.

But Rosso, even though he was blessed with talent and good looks, didn't have much luck. During the sack of Rome, he was captured by the Germans, who stripped him and forced him to lift huge weights and empty a shopful of cheese. Luckily, Rosso escaped and all was well for a time, until he was commissioned to paint a panel picture. In the process of this skilled work, the roof fell in (no, the ape wasn't responsible this time), and smashed the panel. Rosso, understandably enraged, developed a fever that nearly killed him. The postscript to this little tale is that suicide succeeded where the fever did not, and Rosso killed himself.

Fevers were frequently rife in Italy, and, although they usually burned themselves out, in Caravaggio's case, the fever resulted in his death. Not that he hadn't been working up to an early demise. Stabbings, court cases, and murder generally put years on anyone, and he was no exception. His whole life was one long, exhausting argument. He loathed all other painters, dead or alive, because in his opinion he could paint better than any of them, and he was not above writing scurrilous and obscene verses about competitors and pinning them on walls for the further education of the passing populace. He threw artichokes at a waiter, crying, 'Do you take me for some kind of bum?' (That, incidentally, is an accurate quote taken from court records.)

Then he parted his model's lover's hair with an ax and chucked stones at the police for light relief. The way he died was ludicrous. After having been expelled from Rome, then thrown out of Malta for unspecified vices, Caravaggio moved to Port-'Ercole, where he was deposited in prison by mistake. When he was finally released, he was just in time to see his ship set sail with all his goods on board. In a demented attempt to stop it, he ran along the seashore in the blistering heat and then collapsed, dying of fever three days later. The last horrible irony is that his goods were not on board — they had been set aside for safety in the customs house.

Tragedy dogged Caravaggio, but it was humor that shaped Charles Willson Peale's life. This eighteenth-century American artist was one of those gentle eccentrics who lead vivid lives. Mr. Peale's interests were legendary; not content with painting a selection of bigwigs of the Revolutionary War, including Washington, he founded the Peale Museum and exhibited the bony carcass of a prehistoric elephant (an animal with nipple-shaped tubercles on the crowns of its molars).

It was hardly surprising that Peale and the elephant caused quite a stir, and that stir attracted a succession of three wives to Mr. Peale, and seventeen children, all of whom were named after painters: Raphael, Rembrandt, and so on. This lusty gentleman liked women, and when his third wife died, he set about finding a successor — which was how *he* died. (Deservedly so, some might say.) In a valiant attempt to impress his lady love, Mr. Peale, at eighty-six, carried a trunk (a luggage trunk, not an elephant trunk) for over a mile to her house. Unfortunately, his heart gave out with exertion, not passion, and he died minutes after his arrival.

Henri Rousseau felt the burning pangs of love, too. This naïve French artist epitomizes the Sunday painter, discovering his interest after a series of different careers. Having spent some time as a regimental bandsman in Mexico, and as a sergeant in the Franco-Prussian War, he worked as a customs officer in Paris. His interest then turned to painting, although he also taught elocution and music, and considered himself to be something of a playwright. As if this wasn't enough, he even managed to become embroiled in a fraud trial, living up to his label as 'naïve' both in his personal and artistic life. Yet in the end, he died of a broken heart. After he set his sights on a third wife, the chosen lady remained heartlessly immune to his attentions and her indifference killed him.

Fra Filippo Lippi would have understood his feelings well, as he loved women with a passion not usually encountered in clerical gentlemen.

His life began in a spectacular fashion when he was orphaned at two and was then sent to be a friar at a Carmelite convent. But he showed no interest in anything other than drawing, and as he grew up he reveled in the considerable praise his work excited. By the age of seventeen he was not content to stay locked up at the monastery and went absent without leave. Unfortunately, while enjoying himself sailing, he was captured by a Moorish galley and taken to Barbary in chains.

Lippi remained like this for eighteen months until he thought of an idea. (He was a slow thinker.) With charcoal, he drew a portrait of the Master Moor, decked out in his full costume, on the prison wall. The Master was duly summoned to what was possibly the first recorded private showing, and fell about in admiration, heaping portrait commissions on the reluctant friar. In this case, the Moor the Merrier.

And so, in a bound, our hero was free! A little while, and several portraits later, he was finally allowed to leave for Naples, from where he moved on to Florence and the influential patronage of Cosimo de' Medici, and the women . . .

Influential patronage played a large part in Piero di Cosimo's life, too. This Italian painter was born in 1462 and found early fame after moving to Rome. However, as his fame increased, his common sense decreased, and he began to lead a very odd life, turning rapidly into a subhuman. He would not allow anyone to dig his garden or prune his trees, and personally he blossomed under the introxicating influence of Mother Nature.

Not that the seamier side of life escaped him — Cosimo would stand for hours contemplating a wall covered with spittle, telling anyone mad enough to listen that he could see landscapes there. Possibly due to this fevered imagination, Cosimo frequently was employed for masquerades (not to perform but to organize them) and scored a thundering triumph with his 'Chariot of Death.' This chariot was drawn by buffalo, painted with human bones and crosses, and the figure of Death was surrounded by tombs. Later on, just to stop anyone dozing off, the tombs opened up and a good many Hammer Horror look-alikes leapt out, gibbering madly.

Born today, Piero di Cosimo no doubt would have made a fortune working with Ingmar Bergman, but then such spectacles, although admired, had a way of ensuring the creator's exclusion from polite society, and Cosimo's chanting of 'Grief, Woe, and Penitence' didn't help matters. The citizens were amazed and impressed by the 'Chariot of Death' but kept their distance from the inventor.

Cosimo didn't care — he was totally committed to his work and unconcerned about anything or anybody else. In fact, in a fit of exasperation, he called his patron, Lorenzo the Magnificent, *Il Magnifico Merdo* — 'The Magnificent Shit' — a remark that could have resulted in his head decorating the end of a sharp spike.

But because he was regarded as something of

an eccentric, he got away with it and, as time passed, Cosimo became obsessed with his painting, cooking fifty boiled eggs at a time so that he could economize on the firewood and save time worrying about a balanced diet. To quote Vasari, 'He could not stand babies crying, men coughing, bells ringing, or friars chanting.' Yet somehow, Cosimo still managed to reach old age, shouting at shadows and cursing doctors (which only goes to show he wasn't as crazy as people thought.)

Near the end, he had humanitarian thoughts and he took to praising public executions, saying that he thought it was a nice way to go — with all those people around you. He died alone, after falling down his staircase, his house unswept for years, his garden thick with weeds.

Perhaps it was due to the climate that so many of the Italian artists were larger than life, such as Salvator Rosa, the seventeenth-century actor, musician, and artist. This man of many talents started out as a bandit. Painting landscapes in between robbing and looting, Rosa moved to Rome, where he suffered from malaria and had to leave in a hurry to recuperate. He returned a year later and, in a rash gesture, composed a little ditty about Bernini, who happened to be the local bigwig in the artistic community, and a man who combined religious fervor with bloody-mindedness. Not surprisingly, Bernini did not see the joke, and Rosa was persuaded to leave Rome before he fell victim to the Italian virus (poisoning).

No one could stop John Ruskin, the Victorian

painter and critic, from saying or doing anything. His opinion carried weight and his criticism could make or break a painter. He was fascinated by geology and encouraged other like-minded artists, such as John Brett, of whom Ruskin wrote: ' . . . he is much stronger than Inchbold, and takes more hammering: but I think he looks more miserable every day and have good hope of making him completely wretched in a day or two.'

Ruskin was obviously not someone who would have qualified as a Thomson's tour guide and, after reading this letter, perhaps it is not surprising to learn that he died insane.

Théodore Géricault did not, which *is* surprising, as he slept with severed heads in his room. He didn't live long — only thirty-three years — but in that time, Géricault managed to achieve a tremendous reputation both personally and professionally. In fact, he cut quite a dashing figure and had very strong views on everything. He was so angry when Louis XVIII's troops deserted and went back to Napoleon that he joined the Musketeers and helped the King cross the border into Belgium.

Noble as the action was, however, Géricault appeared to undergo a sea change later and sided with the opponents of the restored monarchy, taking artistic potshots at the political events of the day and living a somewhat raddled life, which ended after he fell from a horse.

Jacques-Louis David was famous for his astonishing realism — and his politics. His life was turbulent from the first. His father was killed in a duel and his teacher foiled his chances of winning the Prix de Rome. David became a neoclassical artist and ousted Boucher (a distant relative who had helped him to get started) by painting such stirring scenes as *The Oath of the Horatii*. His own life was a mixture of grand gesture and petty spite. During the French Revolution, David voted for the execution of Louis XVI and abolished the Academy — although, after Robespierre fell, he was put in jail as a reward for his political views. Due to the intervention of his wife, who had divorced him (they remarried later), he was released. He met Napoleon, fawned over him, and became the emperor's painter, immortalizing the ludicrous little (five-foot-three-inch) man in a variety of majestic poses until he was deposed, and David had to flee to Brussels, where he died.

While David was working in France, George Stubbs was painting in England. Born in Liverpool, he was studying anatomy at eight years old — which makes him either a genius or a smartass. Either way, his career was launched and he began working for the Wedgwoods. Unfortunately, Stubbs was soon bored with England and he set off for Italy, on the way witnessing a lion attacking a horse. This happy event was later used as a subject for one of his most inspired and celebrated works.

But Stubbs was not just a painter, he was also an anatomist, and drew horses repeatedly, creating a remarkable portfolio of drawings entitled *Anatomy of the Horse*. For six years, he worked on his task in a deserted farmhouse in

Lincolnshire, and kept dead horses in the studio for weeks at a time, some trussed up on pulleys, others in various stages of decay, heads, tails, and feet in gruesome piles everywhere, like a slaughterhouse.

He may have been a wonderful horse painter, but he was no animal lover. The horses he dissected first were bled to death, after which he pumped their veins up with a solution that hardened them, so that they could retain their shape. With the skill of a butcher, rather than a painter, Stubbs then had the carcasses hauled up on iron hooks, and dissected them muscle by muscle, a procedure that took up to six weeks per horse.

Stubbs did have one human companion, however, a Miss Mary Spencer, who must have suffered either blind love or blocked nasal passages, because she stayed with him and put up with the decomposing remains of the series of dead horses that were flayed, and then gradually stripped of skin, then muscle, until they were exposed down to the bone, their charnel remains hung up like so many soiled goods at an end-of-season sale.

Sir Edwin Landseer was another artist who made a fortune out of painting animals. As a child he soon secured a name and was well known at twenty, showing at the Royal Academy and becoming chummy with the likes of Dickens and Thackeray. His reputation was further enhanced by his becoming a favorite of Queen Victoria and of the nobility, picking up a titled mistress on the way.

Landseer soon fell into the trap of trying to amuse — his painting descended from imaginative animal studies into ludicrous parodies. His patrons loved his work, but his friends did not, and Dickens and others were soon repelled by the assortment of sentimental monkeys and lapdogs that panted down from the walls of the rich.

But however cushy Landseer's professional life was, the course of true love never did run smooth, and in his case it hit a very rocky patch when his mistress's husband died. Not unnaturally, the artist thought that now his love would marry him — but the lady thought otherwise and gave Landseer his marching orders. Rejection is never easy to take, but he reacted so badly that he suffered the first of many nervous breakdowns, which culminated in insanity.

Landseer's temperament was never very sound, and although his drinking accelerated his mental instability, his talent for painting animals accurately, while giving them human expressions and feelings, touched the sentimental Victorian heart and made him a superstar. Landseer's skill for painting animals was, however, at odds with his desire to blow their brains out on shooting trips, and on many occasions he went deer stalking with the good and great, ready to blast any would-be sitter off the hillside.

Maybe this peculiar paradox in his nature explains the sickening cruelty in some of his paintings, as in the picture of the cat holding the monkey's paw into the fire, or in some of the dog fights he depicted. In others, Landseer's mawkish sentimentality shines through, as in *Good Doggy*, a painting not to be viewed on a full stomach. But he *was* a very gifted sculptor, as can be seen from the bronze lions around Trafalgar Square, upon which many a pigeon has passed its own critical judgment.

Landseer's reputation for animal painting was further underlined by his legendary ability to get on with anything on all fours. This, no doubt, was true in most instances, but on one occasion when he was called in to attend a particularly nasty cur, the animal was unimpressed and continued to bare its teeth and bark viciously. Landseer, employing impressive psychology, snarled and barked back — and then watched, astonished, as the terrified dog fled into the distance in blind terror.

Perhaps *The Mask* gave this artist the best epitaph of all, when it stated, 'Not a dog in London but knows him.'

No one knows whether Leonardo da Vinci got on well with animals, but since he could do everything else, it's more than likely. This artist was the son of a peasant girl, but possessed all the advantages of a prince. He was handsome, could sing divinely, played the lyre better than an angel, and generally inspired devotion in everyone — apart from Michelangelo, who loathed him passionately. As if all this wasn't enough, Leonardo was also so physically strong that he could bend horseshoes with his bare hands, could tame wild horses, and fenced like Douglas Fairbanks.

While he was still a child, he was apprenticed

to the talented Verrocchio, and was set to work on his master's picture *The Baptism*, painting the left-hand angel with such skill that it caused Verrocchio, in a rush of typical artistic magnanimity, to throw down his brushes and swear never to paint again if a child could do better than he could.

With youthful high hopes, Leonardo wrote to the Duke of Milan, saying that he could build bridges, make guns, perfect catapults, organize sieges, make tunnels, create sculptures, and paint. He then rounded all that off with 'I recommend myself to you in all humility.'

Possibly due to this astounding lack of confidence, the duke employed Leonardo, and from then on there was no looking back. In the following years, he painted the *Virgin of the Rocks* and the *Last Supper*. When he was working on this, Leonardo's agonizing slowness irritated some of the monks (for whom it was being painted) and some would watch him work and fret about the amount of overtime he was putting in. After days of interruptions and aggravations, one particular monk asked the painter what was holding him up. The artist replied that he couldn't find anyone who looked evil enough to be the model for Judas, although he had walked around the streets and searched everywhere. In such deeply devout times, the personification of the twelfth disciple was vital — he had to represent absolute wickedness.

The following day, the monk returned and asked the same question. In fury, Leonardo threw down his brushes and told the cleric that he had finally found his Judas — if the monk would be kind enough to sit for him!

But that was not the ignominy that the *Last Supper* suffered. Later on, the monks decided that an extra doorway was needed in the refectory, where the painting adorns a wall, and set about amputating Christ's legs and those of several disciples in order to make room for the exit. As if that wasn't enough, during the French Revolution, Napoleon's soldiers entertained themselves by throwing stones at the row of painted heads, picking the saints off one by one like ducks in a shooting gallery.

Leonardo must have been truly remarkable, because one of his patrons was Cesare Borgia, a man who slept with his own sister, poisoned anyone who stood in the way of his political ambitions, and spent his quieter moments devising unspeakable tortures for use in his dungeons. Around this time, Leonardo painted the *Mona Lisa*, whose smug look is taken to mean many things. Some people believe that she was pregnant; others that she was in love with Leonardo; others think she was really a man. The truth, according to Vasari, is that Leonardo employed jesters and musicians to amuse Mona — and thus prevent the boredom that leads to that familiar look of lockjaw present in many portraits.

With commendable skill, Leonardo managed to stay alive under Borgia's patronage and then went on to work for Francis I of France, who, having just invaded Milan, decided that some kind of celebration was in order. Always one with an eye to the main chance, Leonardo arranged the festivities, making a mechanical lion that circled the banqueting room like a Renaissance Dougal, and then stopped in front of the king and flipped open its chest, which was packed with lilies. Impressed by the novelty of a regurgitating lion, Francis grew very fond of Leonardo and even when Leonardo's painting hand became inconveniently paralyzed, he looked after the artist, calling him 'father' and allowing Leonardo to breathe his last cradled in his kingly arms.

Leonardo was accepted and revered; Giovanni Antonio, Bazzi, or Sodoma as he was known, was not. It wouldn't have mattered to him, because this was a man who knew how to enjoy himself; and if Vasari wrote scandalous accounts of his life, well, he saw nothing wrong in living up to such free publicity. His ready wit and warm personality made him very popular and he was friendly with a selection of vastly rich bankers and princes, who could fully appreciate his little foibles.

As Sodoma became more and more success-ful, he indulged his love of the theatrical and kept vast numbers of animals — African donkeys, hens, and Indian turtledoves, to name but a few. Then, just in case anyone failed to notice him when he was out, Sodoma wore garish costumes and rode a Barbary horse.

But oddly enough, this behavior earned him fame and wealthy patronage, his career crowned by a knighthood from Pope Leo X — after which he always was referred to by the remarkable title

Il cavaliere Sodoma. However, although the rich and powerful might have been impressed by him, the taxman wasn't, and on one occasion Sodoma sent back a tax return, stating, 'I have an ape and a talking raven . . . I possess three beastly she-animals . . . and have also thirty grown-up children, which is a real encumbrance . . . and as twelve children exempt a man from taxation, I recommend myself to you. Farewell.'

*　*　*

Sodoma was obviously very interested in sex, as was Rosa Bonheur — but in a different way. This lady was a fine nineteenth-century painter, but if she was clear about her work, she was ambiguous about her sexuality. Painting vast pictures of lusty stallions at horse fairs would have earned her reputation enough, had it not been for the fact that she cut off her hair and dressed up as a man. As this was before the days of cross-dressing, when people still thought it strange for a stocky little woman to dress up as an undersized, stocky little man, Rosa Bonheur had to receive permission from the police to carry on like this. Thus she was permitted 'permission de travestissement,' and allowed to continue frightening the horses.

Guido Reni was not at all concerned with sexual matters regarding dress or affairs of the heart. He lived in Italy at a time when life was morally and politically corrupt — times in which women were valued as courtesans, men were encouraged to indulge in all the vices, and poisoning was a way of determining the pecking order. So you can imagine how this era reacted to the news that Reni was a *virgin*! Nothing could have been worse, or more contemptible, especially as Reni compounded the felony by remaining a *lifelong virgin*.

It was only after the artist began to show some real mettle and became an avid gambler that his contemporaries forgave him. In fact, Reni's addiction to games of chance compensated for his lack of interest in the physical passions and absorbed much of his free time. Caravaggio threatened to kill him, but Reni was clever enough to make sure that he outlived the lunatic.

It would have been quite a meeting if Michelangelo had met Caravaggio, but they lived at different times and went their own ways. Both of them were extremely gifted and yet despite their talents both suffered in their lifetimes. Hounded by Popes, envied by rivals, and often begging for his wages, Michelangelo's life was hard and often lonely. Even his triumphs caused him pain. His magnificent sculpture the *Pietà*, he delivered himself *in a handcart*. And when it was exhibited, one of the many onlookers who had come to view it turned to his companion and said that he didn't believe that Michelangelo had carved it. In fury, the sculptor went back that night with his tools and chiseled his name across the sash on Mary's breast.

Michelangelo's patrons also abused his talents, putting him to useless tasks such as making a statue in snow. As the artist grew older, his vision turned inward and he painted the *Last*

Judgment, showing how the damned were punished according to their sins — as in the case of one lustful sinner, who is being pulled down to Hell by his genitals. Michelangelo was obsessed by God and a desire to achieve true beauty, and yet, even when he died, his end lacked dignity. The Pope wanted the artist to be buried in St. Peter's, but Michelangelo's nephew had his corpse removed at night — wrapped up in a bale of cloth, like a purchase from an end-of-season carpet sale.

★ ★ ★

There is nothing more certain that in order to make someone a legend, he has to be handsome and die young. Giorgione qualified on both counts, his actual name meaning 'Big Handsome George,' and his skill at playing the lute and singing soon made him the fifteenth-century equivalent of Sasha Distel and earned him numerous female admirers. He was also pretty nifty with a paintbrush and his nudes (mostly famous courtesans) are remarkably sensuous, as in *Fête champêtre*.

Giorgione's self-portrait shows us a handsome man with a look of supreme self-confidence brought on by early success. Unfortunately (or fortunately, if you happened to be a rival of his), Giorgione caught the plague and died when he was only thirty-three. *How* he caught the plague is another matter. In a romantic gesture that comes straight out of the pages of Mills and Boon, he visited his adored mistress, who had just caught the infection, and with a reckless gesture that couldn't have pleased his agent, he kissed her — and sealed his own doom.

It was not the kind of gesture in which Tintoretto would have indulged. He was too keen to be rich and successful to let sentiment get in the way. Tintoretto means 'little dyer,' and the painter was called after his father, who dyed fabrics, and from whom he got his love of color. As a child, he was apprenticed to Titian, but with true generosity the older master sacked his pupil when he realized how good he was, and Tintoretto went it alone. Undeterred, he persevered and worked hard, making scores of little figures that he hung from the ceiling and from which he made drawings. He also dissected bodies in the mortuaries.

This gloomy practice was fraught with dangers, as the plague made many corpses contagious, and the heat made the cadavers rot quickly. In fact, when Titian died of the plague, his body was granted a special dispensation and instead of being burned, as most plague victims were, was allowed to be buried in church.

Tintoretto continued to do very well and became a success, although he was impatient and wanted to hurry the process along. So when he heard of a competition being held by a rich brotherhood, he quickly thought up a way of outwitting his rivals, Shiavone, Salviati, Veronese, and Zuccaro. Using considerable guile, Tintoretto managed to get the measurements of the room to be decorated, and while all the other painters were obeying the rules and making dinky little models, he was painting away like a madman. On the day when the models were to be judged, everyone arrived, to find Tintoretto's painting completed and already in place. He won, naturally, and the other artists withdrew, chewing the ends of their brushes.

Tintoretto continued to work frenetically for the rest of his life, until he exhausted himself on the immense *The Last Supper* — after which he developed a bad stomach and expired, completely exhausted after fifteen sleepless nights. But the Tintoretto legend did not stop there. A short while ago, several paintings that had been restored earlier in this century were in need of cleaning. The experts who undertook the work were astonished to discover something painted in the background of the valuable pictures. In the midst of the sixteenth-century religious pomp and ceremony, a restorer had indulged himself, and on a whim had painted in several small figures riding bicycles. Apparently, these modern additions had been pedaling their way across the canvases, unseen, for years.

Hogarth would have seen the joke. After all, he was an artist who appreciated humor and painted it frequently, even though his own start in life was bleak enough. When he was only four, his father, who had been a schoolmaster, opened a Latin-speaking coffeehouse, which, not surprisingly, was a total failure. For the next three years, the family lived in Fleet Prison — an experience that made its mark on Hogarth, and one that often shows itself in his paintings of lowlife.

Like many a patriotic Englishman, Hogarth

also was renowned for his hatred of the French, and his xenophobia wasn't helped when he was arrested in Calais as a spy. (In fact, he was only collecting background sketches for his picture, *O, the Roast Beef of Old England* at the time.) But when Hogarth wasn't abusing foreigners, he was a great champion of justice, and was very influential in later years, helping to champion the Copyright Act, to protect artists' work.

Unfortunately, Van Gogh had no need of the Copyright Act, because no one wanted to steal any of his work. His was a real example of a tragic life, a struggle that probably would have driven anyone barking mad. His first career was as a clerk to an art dealer, but, after a failed love affair, he left the gallery and asked to be accepted into the Church. No thanks, they replied with true charity. But Vincent was not put off and, thinking he had a mission, he took himself off to Belgium to preach.

Soon after this, he began to paint and his life seemed to open up for him as his passion grew. Sadly, no one else was gripped with the same passion to buy, and Vincent was so poor that he often had nothing to eat for days. Not surprisingly, he began to have hallucinations and things went from bad to worse, culminating in a fight with the boorish Gauguin, after which Vincent cut off his own ear in a fit of remorse.

From this point onward, things became a little surreal. Here was Vincent with his ear in his hand, obviously in a state of confusion. After all, what *do* you do with the odd ear? His answer was to send it as a present to a prostitute at a nearby brothel. The girl was heartless and thought the gift in poor taste, and told everyone about it. Soon they all got together, decided that Vincent was off his rocker, and had him carted off to an asylum.

For the following few years, he was in and out of hospitals and asylums, friendless apart from his devoted brother, Théo, who supported him as much as he could. But in the end, it was all too much, and Vincent walked out into a cornfield and blew a large hole in his chest, lingering for two days before finally dying. The sad postscript to this is that Théo died of grief soon afterward.

While poor Vincent never really had much of a chance, Brian Hatton was fêted from the start. This nineteenth-century painter was a child prodigy who was so talented that the great artist G. F. Watts took him under his wing and predicted a brilliant future for him. In fact, Hatton was so cosseted that once, when he was in poor health, Mrs. Watts sent daily telegrams to check on his condition.

But Hatton did not live up to his early promise and his career did not flourish as was hoped, being cut short at twenty-one when he was stationed in Egypt with the army. He sent letters home to his parents, which read more like postcards than tales from the battlefront: 'I am thoroughly enjoying myself . . . One only has to lie down behind a few inches of sand hill to be quite safe from any bullet.'

Many a foolish man has been overconfident and lived to regret it. Unfortunately, Hatton was not one who did. Despite his molelike activities, one stray bullet did manage to find its way through the sand hill and sent him to his Maker only days later.

Hatton was an Englishman and a Victorian, a combination not renowned for its broad-mindedness, and he would no doubt have strongly disapproved of Jean-Baptiste Greuze, who was a Frenchman and a lecher. This artist started off well enough, painting genre scenes that epitomized the best of man, such as *A Father Explaining the Bible to His Children*, but from then on his taste changed, as did that of his patrons, and he turned to the depiction of children, then advanced to suggestive paintings of semiclad young women. Apparently he was incredibly vain and became very unpopular with his fellow artists, who were no doubt delighted by his ill-fated marriage.

Poor Greuze might have enjoyed the pleasures of the flesh, but he paid dearly for them. The pretty model he married cheated him out of his money and ran off without so much as a backward glance.

Thomas Gainsborough liked women, too, but had the good sense not to let them ruin him. He was very successful in his lifetime and his paintings of well-dressed, pretty women and gallant men appeal as much today as they did in his own time. Totally without pretensions, he shunned the pompous artistic circles dominated by Reynolds, and kept to the kind of company with whom he could drink and enjoy a bawdy joke — and a willing female.

Strangely enough, for all the pretty women he

painted, Gainsborough did not care for portrait work and preferred to paint landscapes. However, as tree stumps and cows did not sell well, he wisely concentrated on painting people, knowing that there was only one other artist to rival him: Reynolds. Their feud soon became the talk of London, and the publicity hurt neither of them. Gainsborough's life was marred by only one real shadow; his two daughters, Mary and Margaret, both fell victim to mental illness.

Gainsborough did leave us with one tantalizing tidbit on which to ponder. At the moment of his death, he apparently said, 'We are all going to heaven, and van Dyck is of the company.'

One doubts if there would have been a rush to that particular knees-up.

Gainsborough was not a prude and would certainly not have been shocked by the Dutch genre painters, such as Brouwer and David Teniers, who were remarkable for the earthiness of their work. Peasants relieving themselves in the corners of rooms were in keeping with the times, and even Rembrandt drew a man and woman obeying the call of nature on the roadside. Such manners were not peculiar to the Dutch; in the palace of Versailles the French used to relieve themselves in the corners of the ballroom.

The mistresses of Louis XIV had to find other ways to cope with their bladders. Though the king could go hunting for up to eight hours without urinating, his ladies could not hang on so long — and crossing their legs was only partly effective. So, under the sumptuous gowns

39

painted by the likes of Watteau, they secreted small bottles, thereby ensuring some means of relieving themselves.

In general, the hygiene of most courts left much to be desired. Aside from the men's bad habits, the women wore their high powdered wigs for months on end, using back scratchers to get at the vermin who had set up house in their coiffures.

Clothes, as ever, were a mark of class, but in England clothes became sadomasochistic and began to work against the wearer. In a painting by Gainsborough, *Mr. and Mrs. Andrews* (and Velázquez's *The Infanta Margarita*), the women are wearing dresses whose skirts are so wide that it would have been impossible for two females to pass through a door at the same time without one breaking her pelvis. The bustles so beloved of James Tissot deserve a mention, too. These wondrous contraptions worked on the same principle as a concertina, collapsing when a lady sat down, and then flipping back into place as soon as she got to her feet!

Velázquez would not have found such things amusing. He was far too serious and dour, and seems to have lived his successful life quietly and with a good deal of that famous Spanish gloom. The only insights we have into his character are in his work. Apparently Velázquez did not like to break off when things were going well, not even to wipe his brushes. So when they got too clotted to use, he would wipe them on the canvas to clean them! A perfect example is in the portrait of *The Dwarf Don Diego de Acedo*, 'El Primo,' where the background is covered with long scratch marks, as though a cat had sharpened its claws there.

But gloomy as he was, Velázquez did help other painters. One such person in need of a helping hand was Alonzo Cano, who took over where Caravaggio left off. He spent his life keeping lawyers busy with legal cases and quarrels, flinging his money about like a drunken sailor. As usual, such diversions have a price, and Cano found himself doing a moonlight flit from Seville after one particularly messy duel.

With great good fortune, he happened to be chummy with Velázquez, who, in turn, happened to be chummy with the king. Flinging himself on the artist's mercy, Cano begged for help, and Velázquez, no doubt after some serious moralizing, had the cowed Cano appointed as painter to the monarch. This prestigious position, under the scrutiny of the eagle-eyed Velázquez, effected a miraculous personality change in Cano as he knuckled down to work and calmed down in his private life, finally returning to Granada to enter the priesthood! (Uncharitable people said it was more for the pension than for the love of God.)

It's a shame that Velázquez wasn't around to bring Godfrey Kneller down a peg or two. This seventeenth-century portrait painter was an egomaniac. After training in Amsterdam, he went to England and followed Lely in making a brilliant career for himself, which resulted in his being made a baronet. Kneller's most famous paintings are of the members of the Kitcat Club — which was not an advertisement for Whiskas but a famous London dining club, named after the mutton pies known as 'kit-cats.'

The success heaped upon him made Kneller even more conceited and insufferable, and when the writer Alexander Pope suggested maliciously that God might have done a better job on the creation if He had talked to Kneller first, the artist agreed, and then, looking at the diminutive, hunchbacked Pope, said, 'Obviously some things would, indeed, have been better made.'

Ouch!

Kneller's arrogance must have been quite a shock for the London society that had previously dealt with Sir Peter Lely, a man who was charm personified. This artist was fabulously successful in his lifetime and his reputation for painting languorous, seductive women was next to none. He succeeded van Dyck when he became Principal Painter to Charles II, and although he was a German, Lely became the most important seventeenth-century English painter.

His luck was certainly a lot better than some of his sitters', as Charles I had the dubious privilege of sitting for Lely in prison shortly before his head parted company with his body. Lely must have been adroit, too, because he managed to keep in favor with Charles I, Cromwell, and then Charles II. Wealthy and clever, Lely gathered together a formidable art collection of his own and then painted the famous *Windsor Beauties*. It has never been discovered whether the Duchess of Somerset was breathtakingly beautiful or breathtakingly critical — but either way, Lely expired in a fit of apoplexy when he painted her!

The Grim Reaper strikes painters at some of the most inconvenient times, and Louis Languerre was one who met his end under very odd circumstances. His father was the keeper of the Royal Menagerie at Versailles, which doesn't mean that he had to clean the parrots out but that he was something of a bigwig. This can be further proved by the fact that Languerre junior's godfather was Louis XIV.

With such contacts, Languerre's career was plain sailing. He painted in Hampton Court, decorated Sir Godfrey Kneller's London pad, and worked for Queen Anne — none of which prepared him for his demise. He made a quick entry to heaven while halfway through the first act of a play at Drury Lane.

Turner would have had little sympathy. He was always so involved with his work that leisure pursuits such as the theater were of little interest to him. Joseph Mallord William Turner was the son of a London barber and wig maker. While still in his teens, he worked for the draughtsman Thomas Malton, who insisted (with the kind of insight that loses fortunes) that his pupil had no future. Turner's home life was insecure — his mother's fierce temper turned into insanity — and yet, despite this, he lived at home until he was twenty-four, and remained close to his father all his life. They called each other Daddy and Billy, and although Turner seldom spoke about his family, he once said proudly of his father, 'Daddy never praised me for anything but saving the ha' pennies.'

An unprepossessing man to look at, Turner never married and kept his private life secret, although he obviously had a powerful sex drive, as some of his erotic drawings illustrate. This side of his nature alarmed Ruskin when he went through Turner's papers after his death, and, in a rush of hysterical vandalism, he burned every explicit picture he found.

The real facts of Turner's love life are these: He had two long-standing affairs, one with Sarah Danby, who bore him two daughters and a son, and the other with Sophia Booth, who looked after his Chelsea house when he was older.

While he was still young, Turner was accepted into the Royal Academy Schools (where the pupils could not draw nude female models until they were over twenty or married) and even though he was a strange-looking man, he was frequently lucky with his patrons, such as the marvelous Dr. Monro. This gentleman's practice was very fashionable, and devoted to the mentally ill (it was he who ordered a hop-fiber pillow to treat George III's ravings), and he invited young artists to copy his watercolor collection, offering an oyster supper as a reward for these endeavors. It was here that Turner met Thomas Girtin, after whose untimely death he wrote, 'Had Tom lived, I would have starved.'

But luckily good old Tom expired and Turner became wildly famous, dividing his time between the fashionable country homes of his patrons, his own lower-class family and background, and his secret private life. Turner's work was appreciated, even though he often pushed his luck at the

Royal Academy Varnishing Days. This day was set aside before an exhibition so that the painters could come in and add the last few touches to their work, or varnish it before it was shown. But not Turner — he came in with his paints and brushes and began frantically repainting his picture, so that the canvas that had arrived ended up bearing no resemblance to the one left hanging on the wall.

Cavalier as Turner could be with its rules, he never forgot what he owed the Royal Academy and, on hearing of Haydon's attack on the Academy and his subsequent suicide, he remarked deftly, 'He killed his mother.' For Turner, the Academy *was* his mother, his family, and his first love.

As he grew older, he stopped his constant traveling (although he still walked enough to have his shoes recapped after one day's jaunt) and he remained at home, although it is difficult to see why. Maybe he was immune to the conditions but, although Turner could have afforded to hire a battalion of staff, his Queen Anne Street studio was tended solely by Sarah Danby's niece, a lady who seemed to have an unfortunate aversion to housework. Thick dust covered every surface, the roof leaked, and even the paintings were in deplorable condition. On one occasion, a buyer came in to look at a picture and, because it was so filthy, offered Turner her handkerchief to clean it. In a rage, the artist pushed her away and stood guard over the picture 'like a hen in a fury.'

Turner's secret private life drove many of his

younger colleagues to go to extraordinary lengths to try to trap him. They would offer to walk home with him; he would say he had a meeting or that he was going the other way. They would follow him; he would hide in doorways. In fact, they had a great affection for the old man, who continued to work while drinking heavily in his later years, his false teeth hurting him so much that he couldn't eat solid food.

And when Turner's health finally did fail and the doctor told him he was dying, Turner responded typically and ordered him to drink a glass of sherry and then take another look at him! But it was all bravado — after asking to be propped up so that he could look out of the window at the winter sun, Turner died, the cause being stated as 'natural decay.'

The German artist Albrecht Dürer was another man who took his work seriously. He was interested in everything, from his own body (he drew his self-portrait and then marked out his symptoms before sending it to his doctor) to the careful examination of stag beetles. His career began well when he took out a form of artistic insurance and married his master's daughter, and continued to advance. He traveled widely, studying Latin, mathematics, and geometry, and generally mixing with the fifteenth-century equivalents of Bernard Levin. In this way, his art progressed at a rapid rate and he was elected Court Painter to the Emperor Maximilian.

But all this success was not enough for our hero, and before long Dürer was off on his travels again. Passing a swamp in Zeeland, he was struck by the amazing sight of what appeared to be a dead whale. Not having seen many dead whales in Nuremberg, Dürer wanted a closer look and ploughed his way through the swamp gamely. Unfortunately, he did not catch sight of a whale, but he did catch a fever, and its symptoms dogged him until his death.

Dürer and Turner were lucky in that their work was appreciated; poor old Aelbert Cuyp's was not. He was a seventeenth-century Dutch painter who could turn his hand to anything, painting genre scenes, still lifes, townscapes, landscapes, and portraits. In fact, there are apparently 850 paintings attributed to him. The pity of it is that although he was churning out pictures as if there were no tomorrow, not many people wanted them, and he was forced to take on another job as a brewer to support himself.

Curiously enough for an artist, Cuyp was docile by nature and persisted with his painting even though everyone else was trying to stop him. But virtue, for once, was rewarded, and Cuyp met and married a rich widow, giving up his brewing job in the process. Ironically, when he didn't need the money anymore, Cuyp's work became popular. But success had come too late and he had lost interest in his art, preferring instead his cushy life as a landowning magistrate.

Cuyp wasn't the only one who became impatient with the artistic life. Meindert Hobbema, who painted the world-famous *The Avenue at Middelharnis*, struggled and struggled for success, although he did not marry well and chose the Amsterdam burgomaster's maid, instead. Apparently at thirty, he admitted defeat and threw away his brushes, taking an unimportant job at the Excise instead. After this, he painted very little, and instead of wasting his time creating masterpieces, he devoted the next forty years to measuring wine in barrels.

John Everett Millais never had such problems being accepted. This well-respected Victorian painter was not always so conservative. When he was sent to school, he bridled at the discipline enforced there, making the point with his incisors and biting the headmaster on his third day — his fourth being spent at home. Another thing he objected to was people referring to him as a Channel Islander (which was where he was born), and he would say brusquely, ' . . . being born in the Channel Islands doesn't make me a Channel Islander, any more than being born in a stable makes me a horse . . . '

Millais was actually something of a prodigy and was entered into the Royal Academy Schools at the age of eleven; from then on he was referred to as 'the child.' This nickname stuck, and even when he had grown into a large, rotund, gray-haired old duffer, they still called him 'the child' at his gentleman's club.

Fame came easily to Millais and he was already doing well with his career when another kind of notoriety overtook him. As a good friend of John Ruskin, he had come into contact with Ruskin's wife, Effie, and had fallen in love with her. She returned Millais's affection because her husband all but ignored her and was impotent.

This type of treatment generally leads to bitterness, but how much bitterness was not apparent until, with a blow that must have had Ruskin on the ropes, Effie filed for annulment of the marriage — thus causing excruciating embarrassment to the virginal Ruskin.

This incident became known as the Ruskin Affair and secured a very high profile for all the participants — even the ones who didn't want it. As soon as they possibly could, Effie and Millais married and lived happily ever after, although Queen Victoria would not accept Effie *Millais* having once accepted her as Effie *Ruskin*. As usual, society followed her lead and cold-shouldered Effie, leaving Millais to attend many parties without his wife, although why he had to go at all is a mystery. But finally even the queen bowed to the artist's deathbed request and received Effie Millais at a private audience in Windsor.

It is heartening to think that at the last count they were forgiven by everyone — except perhaps the legion of young boys forced into velvet suits and yellow curls due to the influence of Millais's sentimental painting of his grandson, 'Bubbles.'

Millais's life was one long success, but Canaletto found the going a little tougher. This Italian artist is deservedly famous for his views of Venice, its architecture and its water, each wave crowned with white. Although the young Canale was christened Giovanni Antonio, he was soon referred to as Canaletto ('The Little Canal') and from an early age adored his waterlogged city. In

49

fact, his house near the Rialto Bridge is still standing.

He rose to fame at a speed that would give most people nosebleeds, and benefited from the patronage of such foreigners as the Duke of Richmond, who bought his scenes for their English mansions and recommended him so enthusiastically that before long there was a line around the block of people waiting to buy. With commendable business sense, Canaletto teamed up with the canny Joseph Smith, an unlikable man who became his agent. They also became friends (probably because Canaletto was pretty unlikable himself) and made a great deal of money, although a contemporary referred to the artist as 'a covetous, greedy fellow.'

Undeterred by such sniping, Canaletto kept churning out the pictures and, in order to keep satisfying the demand, employed the help of the camera obscura. This is an instrument that projects an image onto a sheet of ground glass to enable you to trace around it. This neat way of cheating meant that Canaletto could produce a picture in the time it took most artists to squeeze the paint out of a tube, and his work spread across Europe like an architectural plague. Greedy as he was, and successful as he was, Canaletto's career was brought to an unpleasant stop when the War of the Austrian Succession broke out. The tourists who had so eagerly bought his paintings decided that no picture was worth being disembowled for, and they stopped visiting Venice.

Unsettled by this irritating turn of events,

Canaletto left Venice and set off for London, where he was greeted warmly. Patrons bought his works in dozens, but when anyone who was anyone had a Canaletto hanging above the fireplace, they stopped buying. The artist was in a panic and decided that he had better try his luck elsewhere. He returned to Venice. Unfortunately, Venice's fireplaces had enough paintings, too. The war was over, and so was his career. After returning to London again, Canaletto conceded defeat after he was forced to place an advertisement in the paper asking for work.

Nanni Grosso is not a world-famous name now, but it deserves to be. This Italian sculptor was a renowned dandy in his day and appreciated all the finer things in life — even when he was breathing his last. As he lay dying, he was offered a crucifix for comfort. With an aesthetic judgment remarkable under the circumstances, he rallied, and in a vigorous tone told the priest to take it away as it was violently ugly and he wanted one made by Donatello, or he would die in despair! His whim gratified, he passed on happily.

Nicholas Hilliard, the famous Elizabethan miniature painter, had his whims, too. Possibly due to his famous sitters, Hilliard is remembered as the man who painted the likenesses of Raleigh, Sir Francis Drake, and Elizabeth I — who insisted that there should be no aging shadows in her portrait and is now immortalized forever as a regal playing card. Charming and clever, Hilliard became a great favorite at court but taught his pupil, Isaac Oliver, too well, and

51

in later years found himself in rivalry with the cocky upstart.

Hilliard did have his dark side, and for reasons that have never been fully explained, he found himself in the clink, his career cut off in its prime. Luckily, as he was on such good terms with the shadowless Elizabeth, it was only a fleeting visit and he was soon restored to his former artistic prominence.

He did have some curious methods, though. For instance, most painters of miniatures worked meticulously on specially prepared pieces of vellum or ivory. Not Hilliard — he painted on the backs of playing cards and even chicken skin!

Speaking of such things, Paul Gauguin wasn't above chickening out of responsibility. In 1887, this prosperous stockbroker upped and left his family to go native, painting a succession of dusky maidens on various hot islands. He seems to have been a curious man who hovered on the brink of an artistic career before falling wholeheartedly into his art, leaving Paris and going to stay with Van Gogh — a visit that resulted in Gauguin losing a friend, and Vincent losing an ear.

Gauguin did have a vision, though, and was not content to stay with the Impressionists, setting off for Tahiti instead and only returning home when his money ran out. His heart full of hope and his pockets full of cash, he soon set sail again, but had the misfortune to fall into an argument with a bunch of sailors. This is not a course of action to be recommended to anyone, especially an ex-stockbroker, and the seamen set upon Gauguin and gave him a good beating, after which his health was always poor. The rest of his life was spent in poverty and arguments until he died at Atuana at the age of fifty-five, the archetypal tortured, starving artist.

It is not recorded whether Benvenuto Cellini met up with any sailors, but he seemed to meet up with everyone else. This sixteenth-century Italian sculptor was a showman, a man who had the talent of a god and the mouth of a fairground barker. He loved his work, his country, and himself, and did not suffer from modesty — indeed, he believed that everyone should *know* how great he was. Cellini was so committed to his own PR image that he even wrote a book that listed his achievements, pointed out his military heroism, his political murders (he was supposed to have terminated Charles de Bourbon), and, lastly, his amours. With a personality that strongly resembled Errol Flynn's screen persona, Cellini sculpted splendid works such as *Perseus* in between seducing women and saving Italy. Violently passionate about everything, he was also adamant about people and vehement in his dislikes. When he was asked to go to England with Torrigiano, he refused because he could not endure the company of the man who had flattened Michelangelo's nose.

This wonderful example of friendship was one side of his character, the other side landing him in jail on a charge of immorality. (Remember, this was sixteenth-century Italy — you had to be *really* immoral even to be noticed then.) Jail did not agree with him, so with a wily change of heart, Cellini decided to become a priest! Regrettably, he backed out later on, his heart rebelling at the word *chastity*.

El Greco was another artist who didn't suffer from undue modesty. He was born in Crete (hence El Greco, 'The Greek') and, after being a pupil of Titian, went to Rome. With flourishing egomania and no talent for diplomacy, he infuriated countless Romans by saying that if Michelangelo's *Last Judgment* was 'to be cast to the ground, [he] could restore it, honestly and decently, and in no way inferior, as a good painting.'

Such tact soon endeared him to his contemporaries and made success hard to come by. His broody, erratic temperament didn't help, either, and his restlessness forbade him to marry his long-standing mistress, Doña Jeronimo de las Cuevas, whose face looks out from many of his canvases. There is a belief that his elongated, aesthetic male faces are all self-portraits, and that their odd shape is due to El Greco's astigmatism. Certainly the nobility did not care for his eggheaded saints (the artist was accused of 'lunacy'), and the Church became his major patron. But even this lucrative patronage was fraught with difficulties — by buying a house too large and too expensive to run, El Greco constantly struggled to meet the bills and spent much of his valuable time chasing clerics for payment.

The French Impressionists knew a lot about bills, too. Wildly popular today, in their time they were generally regarded as a group of nuts. Manet, Monet, and Renoir all received more than their fair share of criticism and even the gentle Camille Pissarro came in for some censure. Pissarro started out as a clerk in his father's general store, a job that caused him so much heartache that he ran away to Venezuela with a Danish painter to seek his fortune. His parents, by this time convinced of his artistic sincerity, allowed him to try to establish himself as a painter in Paris. Unhappily, his talent was unappreciated, unseen, and undervalued, and Pissarro and his growing family lived in appalling poverty before finally fleeing to London at the time of the German invasion in 1870.

Soldiers are not known for their artistic sensitivity and the Germans were no exception. Pissarro's house literally became a butchery for them, and his treasured paintings were used as duckboards to make a path over the muddy garden (thus making possibly the most valuable carpeting in the world).

Claude Monet had a rough time of it, too. As a young man, he set off for Paris and met up with the other starving artists there. Before long, his father objected to his Bohemian lifestyle, and when Claude refused to return home, he decided on a remarkable course of action. At that time, the army was considered to be a lowest form of life, the bourgeoisie agreeing with Wellington when he pronounced that soldiers were 'the scum of the earth,' and willingly paying vast sums to keep their offspring away from such contamination. But Monet senior had decided that his son was bound for hell in Paris and that he must save him at all costs — so Claude was volunteered for the army.

Algeria is hot and arid. It was even hotter and more arid when Claude was forced to march there with the army, and he loathed the life. But what can't be cured must be endured, so before long he had the good sense to get on friendly terms with the wife of an officer and, after painting her portrait, he enjoyed a reasonable lifestyle. But as luck would have it, just as Monet was coming to terms with Algeria, he became extremely ill with anemia and was sent home.

This time, there was no stopping him, as Claude was hellbent on being a painter. Besides, his father was suitably contrite about the Algerian anemia and agreed to let him go back to Paris with a reasonable allowance jangling in his knapsack. Once there, Claude met artists such as Jongkind, who was an alcoholic and frequently driven insane on binges, and there he studied and there he got very poor again.

But if he didn't find wealth, he found inspiration: He also found a mistress, who bore his child and became a constant irritation to the Monet family. In fact, when Claude was completely destitute, he was forced to stay with his aunt in a ludicrous bed-and-breakfast arrangement — which was all the family was prepared to offer him — and had to leave his mistress and child behind.

Depression took hold of him, and in a letter to Bazille, he wrote: 'I was so depressed yesterday that I was stupid enough to throw myself in the water. Luckily there were no ill effects . . . '

We don't know whether Murillo was a swimmer, but his charming pictures of pretty women and beautiful children seem to show his true nature. After an unremarkable childhood, Murillo was apprenticed to a master, who, after taking his money for the training, promptly backed out. Penniless, the young painter was reduced to painting pictures to be sold at fairs, thus raising enough money to support himself.

But after a while, Murillo's life took a turn for the better and he made a name for himself and married a woman he loved tenderly. Pious and kind, he painted many pictures, including those of the supernatural, and when his wife died, he was left a deeply unhappy man. For years he lived alone, never remarrying, and working without pause, his own existence coming to an abrupt end when he stepped back to admire his work — and fell off his scaffolding! A flight of fancy, no less.

The Spanish people do have a tendency to take things very seriously, and Francisco de Zurbarán was prone to the melancholia of that race. At the beginning of his career, he had the good sense to become friendly with the morose Velázquez, and with great talent and good allies, he became famous. His figures of saints are renowned for their powerful images, though some of his female saints have a rather secular appearance. For example, his St. Casilda in the Prado looks as though someone has had a go at her with lipstick, powder, and paint.

Zurbarán's life hit a sticky patch around the

age of forty-two. His first wife died and he soon married again, his second spouse providing him with enough children to make up a small Welsh choir. Not surprisingly, the artist found it very difficult to concentrate at home, and instead of investigating the possibilities of birth control, he allowed his work to be affected by family life and watched helplessly as other artists became all the rage.

Despite the help of Velázquez and the royal favor conferred on him, Zurbarán disappeared from view. In fact, his life from then onward was clouded by periods of total silence as he withdrew into himself. The end, as they say, was nigh, and one day in a crisis of confidence he threw away his brushes and stopped painting forever.

Professional suicide never occurred to Christoff Paudiss, but jealousy and rage did. These feelings embitter many people's lives but don't usually shorten them. This German painter proved to be the exception to the rule. Having been trained by Rembrandt, he was successful enough to be working for the Elector of Saxony and prospered until his bile got the better of him. All his achievements evaporated when he clapped eyes on a rival's painting, and in the words of a contemporary, 'He died in spite.'

Spite played no part in Luca Cambiaso's life; he would never have had the time for such things. This Genoese painter was always in a hurry. He became famous for his speed and was so fast that he painted using two brushes at the same time. (Before anyone asks, he had one in each *hand*.) In fact, he turned out to be a quick worker in every respect and when his wife died, in order to save time finding a replacement, he married her sister.

So now you have some background on the artists' lives. But there's much, much more. Turn the page and start reading about their patrons, their lovers, their paintings — and what they did to each other.

The Death Toll

Many artists met their deaths with the same violent intensity they brought to their lives, and a vast majority of them died in dire circumstances. They died in duels, in asylums, in the streets, and often by their own hands.

Committed Suicide
Vincent Van Gogh
Giovanni Battista Rosso
Francesco the Younger Bassano
Emanuel de Witte
Mark Gertler
Pieter van Laer
Antoine Jean Gros
Séraphine Louis Seraphine
Benjamin Robert Haydon
Richard Dadd
Ernst Ludwig Kirchner

Died Insane
John Ruskin
Johan Barthold Jongkind
Jean-Antoine Houdon
Hugo van der Goes
Francesco Francia
Maurice Quentin de Latour
John Sell Cotman
James Gillray
Sir Edwin Landseer

Charles Meryon
Roelandt Jacobs Savery

Died of the Plague
Raphael
Giorgione
Titian
Andrea Del Sarto
Michelangelo Merisi da Caravaggio
Adriaen Brouwer
Hans Holbein
Johann Liss
Antonio Correggio

Died Blind
Camille Pissarro
Giuseppe Maria Crespi
Thomas Faed
Hendrick Cornelisz Vroom
Edgar Degas
Sir Joshua Reynolds
Honoré Daumier

Died in Duels
Abraham Bloemaert

Died by Drowning
Andries Both

Died from a Snakebite
Diaz de la Peña

Blown Up
Carel Fabritius

61

Died from a Fall from a Horse
Jean Louis André Théodore Gericault

Died by Falling Off Scaffolding
Bartolomé Esteban Murillo

Died at War
Jean Frederic Bazille
Urs Graf

Died from Cancer
Thomas Gainsborough
John Everett Millais

Died from Heart Disease
Gustave Doré

Died from Tuberculosis
Antoine Watteau

Died After Childbirth
Eva Gonzales

Died from Blood Poisoning
Camille Pissarro

Died from Cirrhosis of the Liver
Gustave Courbet

Died Penniless
Frans Hals
Rembrandt
Jan van Goyen
Francesco Mazzola Parmigianino

Jean Honoré Fragonard
Honoré Daumier
Paul Gauguin
John Crome
George Morland
Jan Vermeer
Cosmè Tura
Jean Baptiste Greuze

2

Eroticism

According to the good old *Oxford Concise Dictionary*, the erotic is 'of sexual love, amatory . . . Gk. erōtikos . . . sexual love . . . ' which is just what we all knew. The fascinating thing about eroticism with regard to *art* is the massive part it played in the artists' lives and in their work.

Take Fra Filippo Lippi, for example. We have already heard how he was captured by the Moors, but his life changed dramatically when he became friendly with the influential Cosimo de' Medici. He was no longer an also-ran, but an artist of some status, and was treated as such. Soon the Pope came to hear of the painter/friar, as did most of the women in the surrounding area. Oversexed and willful, Lippi found it impossible to think about art when his thoughts turned to seduction, and so, in order to keep the artist's mind on his work, his patron, Cosimo de' Medici, locked him in his room! The ruse worked for two days, but on the third evening, Lippi made a rope from bed sheets and set off for a night on the town.

Well, not one night, but several . . . When Cosimo finally caught up with him, Lippi was persuaded to return to work providing that the door was never locked again. For a while, the artist settled and painted happily, but in Prato, Lippi met his Waterloo in the shape of a novice in the Carmelite convent. He swore to have her, but others failed to see his point of view; the lusty friar persisted, but they resisted. Then, in a moment of undivine inspiration, Lippi asked the Mother Superior if he might borrow the novice — and use her as a model in his painting of the Virgin Mary.

With a shortsightedness that bordered on the suicidal, the Mother Superior agreed, and Lippi and Lucrezia eloped the very day she was supposed to be visiting a relic in Prato. Her father fell into an immediate decline, and the nuns into disgrace.

But Lippi must have had something, because Lucrezia remained besotted with him and bore him a son, although he continued to have affairs and to lead a riotously good life, the like of which is rarely seen in an ecclesiastical calling. But luck lasts only so long, and during one particularly sensuous affair, Lippi ate something that disagreed with him (probably because it was poisoned), and expired owing to the not-so-tender ministrations of his mistress's outraged relations.

Sensuality is in the eye of the beholder, or so art experts insist. In the past, most of the religious artists proved capable of great sensuality in their work, and fifteenth-century Italy in particular seems to have been full of friars who were either oversexed or riddled with guilty frustration.

Fra Bartolommeo was one who suffered from the latter. He was misguided enough to become much involved with Savonarola, and became convinced of the ungodliness of his work. So when the notorious auto-da-fé was held in Florence in 1489, he consigned scores of his own sensuous drawings to the flames in a rush of religious fervor. This public display of fanaticism became known as the 'Bonfire of Vanities.'

Unfortunately, the religious fervor did not die out as quickly as the bonfire did, and for the next four years Bartolommeo painted nothing at all and merely concentrated on keeping his brushes and his mind clean. Then, gradually, the lure of the oil paint coaxed him back to the easel, and he set to work. But in the intervening years, many young artists had come into prominence and Bartolommeo was finding it a struggle to get noticed until he thought up a way of proving his superiority. In an irreligious stroke of genius, he painted a wonderfully realistic, and naked, St. Sebastian for a clerical patron and sat back to wait for the response.

The painting was duly hung in the church and immediately attendances went up, the congregation swelling daily, especially among the women. Soon the friars began to complain, saying that the females who came to confession could not keep their minds on salvation while their eyes kept straying up to the gigantic pinup on the wall. In fact, the friars informed Bartolommeo, the painting was forcing their congregation into committing the sin of lust.

The upshot of all of it was this: The artist was told to move his centerfold, or else. Bartolommeo, suitably miffed, did so, no doubt feeling a bit of a fool carrying a naked martyr back to the studio tucked under one arm. But talk of the painting had gone far and wide, and the artist must have been quietly gratified when the St. Sebastian found favor, and a home, with the open-minded king of France.

The French always have been interested in affairs of the heart, and eroticism filtered into many of their works of art — even though sometimes it isn't apparent to the onlooker. Jean Honoré Fragonard worked for a number of important clients, notably Madame du Barry, who unfortunately rejected his erotic series of *The Progress of Love*, thus inhibiting Fragonard's own (progress, that is).

Undeterred, the artist continued to work and quickly found favor with pictures such as *The Swing*. At first sight, this looks like a lighthearted, charming picture, until one delves a little deeper. The Baron de St. Julien had requested it to be painted, asking to have the swing pushed by a bishop, and that 'you must place me where I can have a good view of this pretty little thing.'

This seems innocent enough, except for the fact that in eighteenth-century France women did not wear knickers under their voluminous skirts.

The Italians weren't prudes, either, and Venice was a city that had a very healthy interest in sex. It was a place full to the brim with commerce and in such surroundings merchants flourished, as did the clergy, and artists such as Titian, who relied heavily on the sumptuous beauty of the

Venetian courtesans for his models. He was a man who loved women and sex; his orgies were well known among artistic circles and among princes, his various paintings of Venus apparently illustrating the mistress current at the time. For Titian, a good meal was rounded off by an orgy (which is one way to work off the calories), and sexual displays were watched with interest, the onlookers invited to join in.

As *La Bella* shows, the Venetian women were fabulous and practised prostitution with an openness that was shocking to other European cities. Witty and articulate, they entertained clever men in their salons and gave the same attention to conversation as they did to lovemaking. They were so well accepted, in fact, that they were proud of their profession and walked around bearing the notorious yellow scarf to indicate what they were.

So accepted were they that some of Titian's portraits of these yellow-garbed courtesans were actually an early form of publicity, and this happy marriage of business and art was further advanced when, in 1547, a publication was sold in Venice that listed the courtesans' names, addresses, prices . . . and specialties (the first known edition of the Yellow Pages?).

But not everyone was so keen on sex, and many puritanical euphemisms were bestowed on erotic pictures by prudish collectors. In Munich, the collection at the Hofgartengalerie was only allowed to be seen by *foreigners*, the locals being too unworldly to stomach such things. Even the Viennese gallery managed to convert Palma

Vecchio's *Bella Catta (Beautiful Cat)* from her wild ways, and made her into *The Artist's Daughter*, although God knows what Vecchio would have thought about that. Madrid followed suit, undergoing a rush of priggishness and piling all the bare behinds into a series of rooms that were open only to foreigners (these were the days when it was useful to be a tourist), or artists (who were considered beyond redemption, anyway).

Modesty prevailed to such an extent that the obviously sexual title of Titian's painting of *Donna Lasciva* was altered, so that the sexually predatory courtesan is now *The Artist's Daughter, Lavinia*. Some connoisseurs even managed fabulous flights of fantasy in order to make their collection respectable, and obvious Dutch brothel scenes became paternal rebukes — *A Father Admonishing His Daughter*. In short, for a time, sex was out of fashion.

The Victorians were the most likely people to ban any kind of physical impropriety, even though most men treated their wives appallingly and frequently had mistresses. Yet their very hypocrisy resulted in a rash of morality pictures, the subject of the 'kept woman' being taken on by that goat painter, Holman Hunt, in his painting *The Awakening Conscience* (now in the Tate Gallery, London). In this, we are told that the woman is coming to her senses and repenting her immoral ways as she leaps off her seducer's lap, with her eyes bulging out of her head like organ stops.

Apparently Hunt grubbed around the London

slums peering at the prostitutes to find inspiration — well, that was his story, anyway — although where Ford Madox Brown found his model for *Take Your Son, Sir!* God only knows. Here the fallen, chipmunk-toothed woman faces her seducer (who is reflected in the mirror, music-hall whiskers and all), and holds out their illegitimate child with all the emotion of a waitress handing out a plate of cod and chips.

As a morality story, it fails miserably, just as *The Black Brunswicker* does, although this painting is thought to have two meanings: (1) that the woman is preventing her lover from going to war; *and/or* (2) that he is pushing the door closed behind her, in order to have his wicked way. Its creator, John Millais, always had sex on his mind (possibly due to his dealings with Lillie Langtry), and seems to relish the whole scene, the dastardly Brunswicker and the silk-gowned maiden crushed up to the soldier's top button like a rush-hour commuter. Incidentally, the girl in the picture was Charles Dickens's daughter, Kate, and decorum decreed that the models had to sit at different times, to prevent their meeting, and the possibility of any passions being unnecessarily inflamed.

The pure sensuality of Correggio's *Io* relies on its tenderness to make us believe in something quite ludicrous — that this woman is about to be seduced by the equivalent of a London fog. Real eroticism persuades effortlessly, such as Titian's sensual goddesses, some of whom were painted in front and back views for the king's further enjoyment.

Other artists wouldn't paint such blatant scenes, and hid their eroticism in classical trimmings, numerous works by Lord Leighton and Alma-Tadema displaying yard after yard of exposed flesh in the name of art, carefully arranged draperies making a Roman matron out of a factory girl. Strategically placed peacock-feather fans were much in vogue, too, and marble columns, as numerous goose-pimpled rumps were parked unceremoniously in draughty London studios. The general feeling was that a nude woman with her hair dressed à la Rome was not sexually explicit, while Manet's *Le Déjeuner sur l'herbe* was considered indecent and caused a riot when it was shown, because the models were in contemporary dress.

Eroticism has to be natural to be convincing. Schiele's preoccupation with angles in *The Virgin* has little to recommend it sensually, while Renoir's nudes of his mistress are living, and mercifully free of sentiment. Besides, what is eroticism? Leonardo's drawing of the female vagina? Or Toulouse-Lautrec's sketch of prostitutes up for a VD examination, their skirts held above their waists to expose their nakedness? Or is Rubens the archvoyeur, with his depiction of the mythological lesbian lovers in *Jupiter and Callisto*?

Surprisingly, some of the most startlingly frank drawings were done by the very artists who seemed least interested in sex. Rembrandt, for all his Bathshebas and Suzannahs, is not thought of as an erotic painter. But what about his etching of Potiphar's wife, a lady so sexually amoral that she is even physically deformed? Or the monk making love to a nun in the cornfield? Or the couple making love in the huge Dutch bed? (The woman, incidentally, has three arms.)

Then there is the drawing Rembrandt did of the woman urinating (and worse, if you look very closely), and the paintings Caravaggio did of young boys in a variety of full-frontal poses. Some of these pictures were commissioned by members of the clergy and kept behind locked doors for solitary titillation. Indeed, this painter's picture of St. John the Baptist is blatantly sexually inviting, and the *Lute Player* resounds with all the homosexual leanings of both the artist and his patron, Cardinal del Monte. In fact, the writing on the music in front of the boy reads, 'You know that I love you.'

★   ★   ★

The intense preoccupation with eroticism and homosexuality did not stop there. Caravaggio's painting of the *Boy Bitten by a Lizard* is worrying in itself, the model drawing back in surprise as a small reptile snaps his finger with its teeth. Many murky explanations have been offered to explain this painting, but my favorite is suggested by Alciati, who used the lizard in his writings and who said that the reptile was sometimes used as a method of revenge.

Apparently a deceived wife would grab one of these unsuspecting lizards and chuck it into some wine. After the creature had done a few lengths, the drink was contaminated and, when drunk by her rival, brought her out in a mass of unsightly boils. Naturally, the faithless husband, on being presented with a suppurating mistress, ran screaming back to his wife.

In many examples of early women's liberation, there are numerous paintings that depicted goddesses such as Diana or Atalanta, who, with commendable vigor, managed to obliterate most of the unfortunate men who set eyes on them.

However, not all their victims are put to death on the spot. Sometimes the unfortunate mortal is allowed to challenge the gods in order to win his freedom, as in Guido Reni's *Hippomenes and Atalanta*. This picture illustrates the moment when Hippomenes was engaged in the race with the beautiful Atalanta, who looked like an angel and ran like Sebastian Coe. Unfortunately, as the event continued, Atalanta soon left him for dead. In Reni's version of the race, however, Hippomenes has somehow managed to get into the lead — alas, not for long — soon he is gasping and clutching his sides like a geriatric as the goddess shot past like a Greek equivalent of the Road Runner.

Such mythological tales appealed strongly to the taste of the time. Men and women were sexually adventurous and constantly in competition with one another, so these stories also stimulated their appetites, while providing a convenient excuse to paint nude bodies. To underline the point, many of these paintings were hung in bedchambers, or given as wedding gifts. Others were commissioned secretly by shy patrons or lusty clerics. All religious patrons did not keep their erotic art collections hidden; one Pope even had the gall to have his mistress depicted as the Virgin Mary.

Some mythological characters fared even worse than the exhausted Hippomenes. Actaeon was transformed into a stag because he caught sight of naked Diana — a punishment some might consider a little excessive, especially as he then became a late breakfast for her pack of hunting dogs. Such a story was considered to be titillating at that time, as was the tale of Angelica. This heroine came from the novel *Orlando Furioso*, and she was quite a woman. Unimpressed with the suitors who had come to ask for her hand, Angelica buzzed off to live with a hermit, who, due to his age and general decrepitude, seemed like a reasonably safe bet. Soon the old hermit was foaming at the mouth like a young buck and cast a spell on Angelica to put her into an enchanted sleep. There is a wonderful painting by Rubens that shows the lecherous old recluse pulling back the covers to peer at the naked Angelica.

The painting and the story were a great success, especially as Angelica only managed to escape the hermit in order to fall into worse trouble. Captured and chained naked (shades of bondage here, which was always very popular in erotic art, as were scenes of martyrdom), Angelica was left to be devoured by the sea monster, and was getting understandably worked up when the handsome Ruggiero arrived. He duly unchained her and, because she was stark naked, thought that she should show her thanks in a way pleasurable to both of them. Angelica, however, thought otherwise, and, in a staggering show of ingratitude, ran off to be wooed by a wounded Moor — who was obviously moor to her liking.

Caravaggio never had much truck with female heroines, and preferred his love objects to be male. His *Victorious Love* was very much appreciated by its patron, the Marchese Vincenzo Giustiniani, who adored his full-fronted invitation to a homosexual dalliance. But the picture was too much for some tastes and was separated from the marchese's other works and placed behind a green silk curtain (not a plain brown wrapper), to be viewed only by special visitors.

Many of these erotic paintings were employed in a kind of artistic foreplay, their function being akin to that of *Playboy* these days. Others were commissioned to underline the danger of sexual infatuation. Caravaggio's *Judith and Holofernes* is a good example. Judith was an Israelite who could best have been described as formidable. After her country had been overrun by the Assyrians under Holofernes, she decided that enough was enough and set about destroying the tyrant. After she had seduced him, Holofernes was exhausted and fell asleep — which was when Judith seized her chance, and her chopper, and cut off his head! The painting, like the story, is memorable, but Caravaggio's version is unforgettable because although Holofernes looks suitably surprised, Judith has all the detachment of a grocer's assistant slicing a quarter of boiled ham.

Yet the moral is obvious to a homosexual client — women are dangerous and emasculate men. The point was even more explicitly put in the drawing *Nymph Mutilating a Satyr*, after Primaticcio, in which a woman is actually castrating the bound and struggling male. This is a startling work, which underlines men's fear of women, and is therefore unlikely to have been commissioned by a man. Another painting that elaborates the theme of female dominance is *Salome* by Francesco del Cairo, in which the woman swoons, sensual and fulfilled, before the head of the man she has destroyed.

But all these paintings rely on some background knowledge, whereas Aubrey Beardsley's *Lysistrata* relies solely on our ability to look, and look again. This is a drawing underladen with erotic imagery and, as such, becomes faintly sickening. His work *Messalina* is notorious, too, not only for the illustration but for the sitter, who was supposed to have had sexual intercourse with over three hundred men in one day — for a bet.

Some other attempts at eroticism become ludicrous because they tried too hard: The painting *Gabrielle d'Estrées and the Duchesse of Villars* is one case in point. It shows two naked women, one of whom is delicately grasping the nipple of the other. It should be a disturbing piece, but the action is committed with such indifference that she could be doing nothing more than trying to find her favorite program on television.

But sexual tastes change according to the

times, and in the days of Prince Napoleon Bonaparte, there was less overt eroticism in painting. In fact, when Ingres tried to make him a present of his work *The Turkish Bath*, Napoleon's wife rejected it on the grounds that it was morally decadent. Embarrassed and humiliated, Prince Napoleon was forced to commission a self-portrait instead.

Not that nudity is always decadent or sensual. The famous painting by Georges de La Tour, called *The Flea Catcher*, is a superb example of uneroticism. The woman is virtually naked but, engrossed in crushing the insect between her two thumbnails, she seems superbly undesirable to the onlooker. Indeed, on studying the painting at length, the only real emotion it evokes is a sudden desire to scratch.

But no one was more practical about matters of the heart than the Dutch, and much of their genre painting is taken up with the subject of procuresses, brothels, and money exchanged for sexual favors. The painting *Soldier Offering a Young Woman Coins* by Terborch is an example of the exchange of money for sex, although in this case the woman appears to hesitate, her virtue *and* her asking price in the balance.

There is no hesitation in the painting *Sleeping Woman* by Jacob Duck. The message couldn't be clearer if the artist had put it up in neon lights. The woman is asleep in a chair, while a man sleeps behind her in a position that would usually result in a slipped disk. The presence of the third woman, who is trying to waken the man, adds to the aura of coarse lust. So blatant was the message of exhausted sleep after sexual intercourse that the exposed breasts of the sleeper had been painted over, and the straying hand of the other woman was virtually obliterated until recently. Other paintings by Duck are equally blunt, the *Scene from the Bawdy House* and *Interior with Sleeping Woman and Cavalier* both dealing with sex and lasciviousness.

Mind you, for real eroticism, the picture *The Temptation of St. Anthony* by Domenico Morelli is hard to beat. The besieged saint sits huddled, his cowl half covering his face, his eyes staring straight ahead as a highly charged, bare-breasted female snakes toward him from under a mat.

The blistering sexuality of the painting is as potent as the tame academic nudity of Waterhouse is impotent. Compared to Morelli, Waterhouse's women are beautiful but too immature to be femmes fatales. In the *Siren*, the mermaid entices the sailor to his death with the look of a schoolgirl puzzling over a chemistry experiment. Compare this to Herbert Draper's *Ulysses and the Sirens*, where the sea nymphs creep out from the sea toward the transfixed sailors, whose ears are stopped with wax (not a sign of filth but a tactic they employed to prevent their hearing the dangerous sirens' song).

Legend offers many subjects that seem erotic. *Roman Charity*, by Matthaus Stomer, illustrates the story of the old man who had been left to starve in prison, and whose daughter visits him daily and feeds him with her own milk. Similar stories have been painted frequently by artists, for example *Lot and his Daughters*.

The story goes that after the destruction of Sodom and Gomorrah, Lot and his daughters set off (leaving their mother, who had just been turned into a block of Cerebos), to make a new life. Soon the daughters began to plot and then join forces to get their father drunk, after which they seduced him so that he could have the son he wanted and they could be sure of the continuation of their line — all of which sounds like little more than a very thin excuse for incest.

Incest was a subject not off limits to artists, and certainly many of them had a healthy interest in sex — in all its forms. The sculptor Clodion was used to depicting erotic scenes such as *Nymph and Satyr* for his clients, but after a while he found himself becoming more and more interested in eroticism, and he spent a great deal of his time modeling explicit sculptures of sexual practices best described as deviant.

Some of the artists even portrayed *themselves* in very iffy circumstances. Lanfranco's *Boy on a Bed* is a toe-curling scene of invited seduction, powerfully erotic to a homosexual taste; and Caravaggio posing in a self-portrait as Bacchus has that undulating, self-possessed look of someone who is long past innocence. Yet for some, eroticism is considered more exciting if it concerns forbidden passion. Egon Schiele's painting *A Cardinal Embracing a Nun* panders to a taste that revels in forbidden fruits, even though the sexuality is restricted to the male, the nun looking out of the picture with an expression of bewildered boredom.

However, there is one artist who never needed an excuse to paint something sensual. Rubens looked for, and found, sensuality in everything, and glorified his second wife with a sense of superb satisfaction. *Hélène Fourment in a Fur Wrap* shows her in all her glory, her nude body draped in a fur. Yet instead of a catwalk model, we are offered dimpled knees and a full belly, and even bunions caused by the shoes of the day.

Painters such as Hogarth used their skill to reflect the times in which they lived. In his day, London was rife with crime and prostitution, so much so that Hogarth used both subjects in his paintings. In fact, some of the most famous scenes of prostitution were painted by him. In *The Harlot's Progress*, we trace the life of a young woman who comes to London and is immediately employed by a madam for prostitution. The interesting thing about this painting is that the figure standing in the door of the public house is Colonel Francis Charteris, a notorious dissolute, who is being accompanied by a pimp named John Gourley. Both were well-known figures in the capital's lowlife and roamed the streets in the 1730s, encouraging, and engaging in, the prostitution trade.

In the second painting of *The Harlot's Progress* series, the young woman is already deceiving her rich Jewish protector, and is distracting his attention so that her secret lover has time to escape. But apparently the ruse failed, because in the next painting she has fallen on hard times; indeed, the broom in the back of the picture suggests the service of flagellation, which she now offers. The next scene shows the harlot in Bridewell prison, among every kind of criminal, and the next shows her back on the streets, working as a prostitute.

Unfortunately she now has syphilis, and the mercury treatment has made her teeth drop out. (You can even see them on the paper on top of the coal bin.) Neglected and cold, her child huddles by the fire as the nurse sorts out the clothes she will later steal. Poverty is creeping up on them and so it comes as no surprise that the last painting is of the harlot's funeral. Hogarth shows us exactly how it was in his day: the lascivious cleric overturning his brandy glass in his sexual excitement, and the hideous old madam hovering nearby. This portrait actually depicts a notorious procuress who was well known in London, and who would have been recognized by many of the people who viewed *The Harlot's Progress*.

Hogarth was drawn to scenes of debauchery, his own attitude about sex alternating between detached disgust and real sympathy. In his series of *The Rake's Progress*, he was actually attacking the class of men who were well known to London — the rakes who pursued pleasure and sex with great determination, and little sense. This series of paintings shows the familiar decline of the hero, but there are many fascinating details to be observed on the way. The first picture shows the rake inheriting a fortune, while the mother of the maid he has seduced tries to force him to marry her daughter.

The situation goes from bad to worse and before long the rake is being preyed on by the kinds of people who populated eighteenth-century London. Even the places themselves are painted accurately by Hogarth, the notorious Rose Tavern showing us what such fleapits were like. This place was a whorehouse where rakes would rest up after having flexed their muscles attacking the nightwatchmen who tried to keep law and order in the streets. In this picture, we can again see the mercury pills that indicate that the rake already has the pox, as do the whores who surround him, their faces covered with the black beauty patches that covered either sores or the marks of the smallpox. As the story progresses, the rake is arrested for debt, and although the maid he originally seduced pays his debt, he rewards her by marrying an ugly old woman with one eye, whose physical shortcomings are miraculously outweighed by her fortune.

In Hogarth's day, it was not uncommon for a pregnant woman to make a 'denunciation'; she would call a man in front of a magistrate and swear on the Bible that he was the father. This was a very neat way of securing the illegitimate child's future, as the magistrate would then fine the so-called father and force him to give maintenance. The intriguing thing was that often the men who were denounced were totally unknown to the woman! So it was in her best interests to pick not the most handsome but the most wealthy provider. This efficient means of securing child benefit is beautifully illustrated in Hogarth's *The Denunciation*.

All of Hogarth's paintings depict life as it was in reality, and often the characters he illustrated were based on real people because he wanted to show the world as it was, emphasizing the bad and the evil — and sex was one of the main targets, as it corrupted the innocent and lazy and led to moral destruction. His eroticism had a purpose: to depict sex at its basest, giving his viewers a warning that the physical pleasures lead not only to destruction but also to death.

Nineteenth-century Americans hardly would have been interested in his moralizing. They were incredible prudes. Among museums, the Pennsylvania Academy of Art was notorious for its priggishness. This renowned institution even had separate visiting days for men and women. A collector in another state actually employed a man who spent his whole career making fig leaves. These 'modesty coverings' were stuck on the relevant parts of ancient statues, although some nude figures had to be completely veiled.

It took an English artist, Robert Pine, to set the cat among the pigeons; when he brought a statue of Venus to Philadelphia, the shock waves nearly reached Canada. In hushed tones, he was asked to remove the nude from sight — and out of sight it remained, hidden in a trunk, coming out only to be viewed by the lucky, incorruptible few. Indeed, it took some time for Americans to catch up with the European love of the nude, although at times the English clergy (unlike their Italian counterparts) could be very prim.

After seeing the *Venus* by Alma-Tadema, the Bishop of Carlisle was heard to remark that his imagination had been 'considerably exercised' by the young model. But if the bishop was suffering from palpitations, the flesh painters remained sexually aloof from the naked women they immortalized. Both the bachelor Lord Leighton, and the timid William Etty, were apparently sexually immune — possibly they had developed the same kind of lack of interest ice-cream sellers experience when constantly faced with tubs of dairy vanilla and chocolate. A form of familiarity breeding contempt?

Tales of the white slave trade always have been well received, and when the artist Gérôme visited the Orient, he found many subjects to capture his imagination. Possibly due to his own romantic troubles, Gérôme was fascinated by slavery, bondage, and female violation, and in his painting *The Slave Market*, he shows us a nude woman being bought by a nineteenth-century version of the desert prince. Surrounded by gawking men, the slave girl allows her would-be buyer to insert two fingers into her mouth to check on her teeth. The principle of the slave market was that women could be bought, or sold, young virgins fetching the highest prices. It was a curious form of barter that appealed strongly to some men, and was especially titillating to the Victorian taste.

But if subjects like the slave trade were obviously sexually exciting to their patrons, others enjoyed looking for *hidden* meanings in paintings. In Dutch painting, for instance, a dead

84

bird means much more than is at first apparent. Apart from having come to a very nasty end, the fallen fowl alludes to the Dutch word *vogelen*, which means 'to bird' and 'to copulate.' Other household objects have salacious meanings, too — tankards and mugs symbolize the womb; candles, carrots, and pestles are phallic symbols; and empty bird cages mean that the bird has quite literally flown and that the sitter is a fallen woman. Cleaning out the budgie will never be the same again.

The Dutch had their own ideas about birth control as well — the carrot was thought to prevent the arrival of a child, and the lowly onion was considered an aphrodisiac. (I would have thought it would have been the other way around.) In fact, the Dutch took many household objects and turned them into amorous symbols — even the mousetrap was thought to symbolize love, as the mouse is trapped with sweetmeats the way a man is trapped by love.

Perhaps the last word on eroticism must go to a painting in the Tate Gallery, London. This is one of the most disturbingly sexy pictures I've ever seen, and has a kind of creepy sensuality that burns into the memory like a cattle prod. It is called *Lydia* and depicts a very young girl, in a very large cap, in bed with her breasts exposed and a distinct 'come hither' look in her eyes. Pretty tame, you might think, and you might even be right — until you read the label, which says painted by Matthew William . . . the *Reverend* Matthew William.

Heartbreak

Artists seem to endure a fair amount of lovesickness and bereavements. Many of their heartaches we have already heard about, but here are a few others.

Dante Gabriel Rossetti
disinterred a manuscript poem from his wife's coffin, *seven* years after she had died.

Ford Madox Brown
lost his first wife, who died on her return from a Roman holiday they had taken. When he married again, his second wife died also.

Ralph Earl
deserted two wives. (The heartache in this case happened to be on the women's side.)

Peter Paul Rubens
Peter Paul Rubens was heartbroken when his first wife, Isabella, died, and later married his much loved, much younger bride, Hélène.

Jean Francois de Troy
died of grief at having been parted from his mistress.

Emanuel de Witte
married twice; his second wife caused him great

distress, as did his daughter. Both of them were convicted of theft and caused him such misery that he committed suicide.

John Ruskin
endured a fiasco with Effie, but he also loved and lost his Irish ladylove, Rose la Touche. When she died, he established the May Queen Festival at Whitelands College, Chelsea, in her memory.

3

Crime

Whatever politicians tell us, crime was not invented in the twentieth century. Like prostitution and taxation, crime was flourishing centuries ago, and was possibly more a part of most people's lives than it is today. Artists, because they moved in what are best described as picaresque circles, found themselves frequently on the wrong side of the law.

In Spain in the sixteenth and seventeenth centuries, forgery was something of an art form, so much so that a painter called Francisco de Herrera decided, after designing some medals, that by forging money he could soon be coining it (so to speak). For a while, all went well, until he was discovered. In the time-honored tradition, the culprit made for the Church, taking refuge in the Jesuit's College. Cringing with guilt, and desperate to return to Philip IV's favor, he painted the monarch a picture, which was duly dispatched to the king while Herrera waited uneasily for a response.

All was well. Philip liked the picture and Herrera was free to roam the streets at will. All might have continued well, had it not been that Herrera was a nasty-tempered man, much given to violence. One by one, his children ran away from home, one daughter (with superb irony)

88

going into the Church to avoid her father. Herrera's criminal leanings, although permanently curtailed by the threat of Philip's dungeon, passed down to his son, and in a parting gesture the last heir not only ran away from home but took his father's savings with him. The biter bit, so to speak.

But forgery is one thing. Herrera chose to be a criminal — whereas some other painters were more sinned against than sinning. Reynolds's girlfriend, Angelica Kauffmann, was already proficient in painting, music, and languages at an early age. Unfortunately, although she was academically bright, she was a dolt emotionally. In 1766, she went to England, after marrying the Swedish Count de Horn, pretty puffed up with self-importance and thinking she had made a good catch.

But very shortly afterward, the rosy glow of satisfaction was replaced by the hot blush of embarrassment, as the Count de Horn turned out to be a *counterfeit*. He was not a member of the aristocracy, he was a *valet*. And there was worse to come — he wasn't just any old valet, but the valet to the *Count de Horn*. For the handsome sum of three hundred pounds, the valet was paid off and bolted back to Sweden, leaving the mortified Angelica seeking solace in the arms of the deaf Reynolds.

Forgery and deception are certainly criminal activities, but they do not compare with murder. Several artists have fallen off the edge to commit murder and not one of them has benefited. Dirty and a braggart, our old friend Caravaggio might have secured himself a place in history on these attributes alone, were it not for the fact that he played tennis. This sport, as we have seen to superb advantage at Wimbledon and Flushing Meadow, soon reveals the competitor's true nature. Apparently, the same was true in early seventeenth-century Italy. After playing a match that he lost, Caravaggio quarreled with his opponent, stabbed him — advantage Caravaggio — and then fled to Naples, after which he spent the remainder of his life in a heady succession of arrests, jailings, and escapes.

Alfred Stevens was driven into a life of crime. This English painter showed early artistic talent and was befriended by a clergyman who put him on a ship bound for Naples when he was only sixteen years old. Speaking no Italian and without any funds or any form of protection, Stevens was soon keeping very bad company, and unluckily became embroiled in the political intrigues that were rife in the nineteenth century.

This artist was a born survivor, however, and stayed on in Naples until things finally got too hot for him, and he left — *walking* to Rome to seek his fortune there. It is to his credit that he then turned away from crime and supported himself with his painting, before finally returning to London — to give the vicar a piece of his mind.

By contrast, the seventeenth-century artist Bernardo Strozzi's paintings are lush and colorful, and betray little of his erratic history. Made a Capuchin friar at the age of seventeen, he was allowed to leave the order to support his widowed mother. This was something at which he excelled, as he became more and more successful. Unfortunately, when his mother passed on twenty years later, the friars wanted Bernardo back. Understandably, he was not eager to go, so he did a runner. In the days when the Church was fabulously powerful, this was a heinous crime and the order and the Papacy did not fall about laughing when they heard the news. In fact, they set off in hot pursuit after the reluctant friar. A series of kidnappings then took place, followed by several furtive escapes in various ludicrous disguises. In a last-ditch attempt at freedom, Bernardo fled to Venice, which was a very wise move — because five years later he was made a monsignor, and lived on happily for another nine years under Venetian protection.

It is debatable whether violence is caused by the times in which people live or by their behavior. Nothing excuses Domenichino's desire to send Lanfranco into the next world, but his action has to be viewed in the context of the artistic life in seventeenth-century Italy. Having to share a commission meant having to share a fee, and that was never popular.

Not long after Domenichino's joint project with Lanfranco was completed, the former moved on to Naples to find new work. Unfortunately, a nasty surprise awaited him there, too. The atmosphere was full of deceit and violence when he was invited to paint the chapel of the cathedral, a job that the Church had been trying to pass off for months. None of the top

Roman painters would touch it, because if they did, they would come up against the local Neapolitan painters, who resented strangers. They already had seen off several notable visitors, and the virginal Guido Reni had beaten a very hasty retreat after one of his assistants had been unceremoniously bumped off.

Domenichino, however, was made of sterner stuff. He not only took on the job but stuck to it, a paintbrush in one hand and a knife in the other. These circumstances would have been enough to try anyone's patience, but then, to rub salt into the wound, his old rival Lanfranco turned up. For the next *ten* years, they were competitors, painting together, fighting together, and beating back the Neapolitan cutthroats, until Domenichino finally expired.

At least both of them were paid. Some artists had to beg for money, such as El Greco and Michelangelo; others squandered what they had. It is a strange fact, but artists and money don't mix. They either can't make it, lose it, or waste it. Take Duccio, for instance. He was going very well and moving up the ranks nicely when he got involved in politics, his sympathies resulting in his being very heavily fined. Considerably poorer, he had the sense to keep his thoughts to himself for a while, but five years later he was at it again. Refusing to kowtow to an official, he was fined once more, and seven years after that he was fined for incurring debts. By this time, Duccio was chastened and kept a very low profile for quite a while, until he refused to join the army — another fine!

You would think there were only so many things for which he could have been fined, but Duccio expanded his talents, and the next time he was fined for sorcery. Curiously enough, this charge did not stop the Church from commissioning the artist to paint something for the cathedral in Sienna, and, due to this Christian intervention, Duccio even began to settle down.

George Morland never settled down. By the age of ten, he was exhibiting at the Royal Academy and his reputation grew — as a painter and as a dissolute. Careless with money, he ran up staggering bills and developed his leg muscles nicely by outrunning his creditors. Dodging and weaving, he managed to evade most of them (even though he was once arrested as a spy), and, if apprehended, he would dash off a quick masterpiece to appease the butcher, or tailor, or landlord. But time, or arthritis, caught up with him and he expired in poverty and prison, his creditors hanging over him to the end.

Parmigianino met his end in a cell, too. Mind you, it seems a great shame that having been captured and having then escaped from the sack of Rome, he was dim enough to be imprisoned for the simple matter of breaking a contract. It was a cut and dried case: Having been employed to fulfill a commission, Parmigianino did so little work that the overseers sacked him, and then had him arrested. Apparently the artist thought that such treatment was unjust, and according to his contemporary Vasari, he turned into 'a bearded, long-haired, neglected wild man.'

His deterioration cut no ice with the

authorities, and Parmigianino died in prison a year later — 'interred naked, as he had wished, with a cross of cypress planted on his breast in the grave.'

★ ★ ★

Politics has been the undoing of many, although nowadays heads aren't cut off. Unfortunately, things weren't so simple in eighteenth-century France, as Girodet discovered. This artist studied under David, and lived to regret it when he became involved in his master's political interests. These interests became so controversial that they caused a riot in which the mob, whipped up to a frenzy, descended on the Academy and ruined it — killing a French agent on the way. With commendable insight, Girodet decided to leave France and remove himself to Naples. But unfortunately, his republican sentiments were not appreciated there, either, and he fled once more.

His flight was hazardous and when he arrived in Genoa, Girodet was extremely ill. But then fortune smiled on him and he came under the protection of the artist Gros (the slave-market painter), his work flourishing as his politics faded. Girodet's greatest claim to fame probably rests with his infamous *Danaë*, a picture that portrayed a well-known whore, whose lover was painted with her — as a turkey-cock!

At this point, well known and successful, Girodet was further blessed by a large legacy. He promptly abandoned his painting and, closed off

94

in a large house that was deprived of any natural daylight, he began to write unintelligible aesthetical poems. Suffocating as this might seem, Girodet apparently flourished in this novel environment, and lived for a further twelve years on a diet of darkness and songs.

Girodet's notoriety came with his amusing *Danaë*, but Géricault's most famous work was altogether more serious. *The Raft of the Medusa* illustrates an infamous event in the early years of the nineteenth century when a number of men drifted at sea for several weeks on a raft, after their ship, the *Medusa*, was wrecked. When their food and water ran out, they began to eat the dead, then the nearly dead, then the far from dead. No one ever knew the real facts, but the painting and its shadow of cannibalism has held a grim fascination ever since.

The Inquisition holds a grim fascination, too, although it was never known for its broad-minded approach, as the Italian painter Veronese found to his cost. Heresy was considered a fiendish crime and was severely punished, many vile tortures zealously employed to fight this evil. At a time when the Inquisition wielded tremendous power, Paolo Veronese was working on his fabulous depictions of religious subjects, such as *The Finding of Moses*. These pictures are remarkable in that the women he used as models were mostly courtesans, and were all dressed in the sumptuous Venetian costumes of the day.

Although Caravaggio got away with using a whore dragged out of the River Tiber for his model of the Virgin Mary, Veronese fell foul of the Inquisition with his next painting. This huge creation, entitled *The Last Super* (later renamed *The Marriage at Cana*), included dogs, monkeys, nosebleeds, fighting cats — and was a little too merry for the Inquisition's taste.

Yet one can see their point. Poor Christ is thrown in almost as an afterthought, pushed right to the back of the festivities like a football supporter straining to watch the game from a bad seat. He also has what appears to be a small band playing in front of him, with Titian on the double bass, Bassano on the flute, and Tintoretto and Veronese on the viola. Behind them sit Eleanor of Austria, Francis I, and Queen Mary of England, together with Charles V of France, and the Sultan Soliman I. There is even a woman using a toothpick thrown in for good measure. In short, if Veronese hadn't given Christ a halo, the onlooker would have needed a map marked with an arrow pointing 'He is here' to find Him.

Not surprisingly, when the Inquisition saw the full extent of *The Last Supper*, they hauled Veronese before them to begin their interrogation for heresy. (What follows is an accurate transcript.)

INQUISITION: What signify these men armed and dressed in the German style?
(*A reasonable question, as the Last Supper took place in the Holy Land, not Berlin.*)
VERONESE: We painters take the same licence as poets and fools and I have depicted these halberdiers ... because it seemed to me

suitable that the master of the house . . . had such servants.

INQUISITION: Who are the persons you admit to have been at this Supper?

(*Trick question, this — answer wrong and you have your tongue pulled out for heresy.*)

VERONESE: I believe there were Christ and His Apostles. [*Phew*] . . . but when I have a little space in a picture, I fill it.

(*He certainly did — with 102 guests, four dogs, two cats, one falcon, and a puppy on the table!*)

INQUISITION: Does it seem suitable, in the Last Supper . . . to represent clowns, drunken Germans, dwarfs, and other foolery?

(*A loaded question. If Veronese had answered yes, it would have looked as though Christ was a lousy judge of character.*)

VERONESE: Of course not!

INQUISITION: Then why did you do it?

VERONESE: I did it supposing that these people were outside when the scene was happening.

(*Having just arrived in several coaches, I suppose.*)

INQUISITION: Can you prove to us that this picture is correct and decent?

VERONESE: My very illustrious lords [*a bit of crawling there*] . . . I hardly took so many things into consideration. I was far from envisaging such disorder.

The upshot of the whole interrogation was that Veronese was told to change his painting, and alter the title to *The Marriage at Cana*; then he had to wipe out the dwarfs, obliterate the fools, and sober up the drunken Germans (a tall order — even the Inquisition would have had trouble seeing to that). In this way, Veronese escaped with his reputation and his tongue intact, dining out on the story for the rest of his life, his popularity secured. The Inquisition never caught up with him, and he was called to his own Last Supper after catching a chill when walking in a procession.

The Inquisition terrified everyone, but in England, murder remained selective. England was a perilous place in Hogarth's day, but, as some of his sitters show, they were very well equipped to deal with the times. Apparently it was also difficult to get good help then, and the famous painting *Sarah Malcolm*, in the British Museum, London, shows us the dire results of hiring someone without references. There is little at first sight to indicate that this maid killed three women, strangling two and cutting the throat of the third, but when Hogarth went to Newgate to paint her, he came away saying, 'This woman by her features is capable of any wickedness.'

Yet because Malcolm was young and reasonably attractive, her story caught the popular imagination and, when she was hanged, they erected a special gibbet for her in Fleet Street (a little innovation that could have been put to good use if they'd left it there) so that Londoners could watch Malcolm's last moments. Her fascination was such that, even after she was cut down, people paid to see the corpse of one of the most hated murderers of the day. And it didn't stop there, because next the medical men got in on the act. After a few days, her cadaver was dissected — and then preserved in a glass case like a British Rail sandwich.

All crime did not involve gain or sex. In the eighteenth century, politicians stooped even further than they do today and pursued everyone this side of the grave for a vote. So we see the blind, the imbecilic, and the ill lining up to vote in Hogarth's picture *The Polling*. But if politics was corrupt, so was sex, and a further allusion to the tastes of the day is shown in *The Death of the Earl*, in which there is a painting of a prostitute holding a riding whip, with which she controlled her unruly visitors!

Although prostitution could be profitable, it could also lead to prison. Due to the fact that many of the plates for *The Harlot's Progress* were destroyed by fire, we have to look at the few remaining engravings for Hogarth's full account of the tale. In one engraving, *Scene in Bridewell*, we are shown in grim detail the conditions which many unfortunates suffered. According to the story, the harlot has ended up in a workhouse, the overseer forcing her to work, a riding whip in one hand providing a neat reminder of the harlot's earlier use for such an article. Behind both of them stands a woman with her hands in the stocks, her arms outstretched upwards, the immortal line 'Better to work than stand thus' written overhead.

There is a variety of people in the workhouse, as there would have been in reality — a dandy forced into labor, a stout woman searching her clothes for lice, and a trollop pulling on a pair of filthy stockings with holes in them, her face bearing the telltale black patches to cover the symptoms of her disease.

Hogarth wasn't the only artist who scrutinized crime and its aftermath. Goya's dark nature was fascinated by tales of cannibalism during the Revolutionary War. At such a time, vile atrocities were commonplace, mutilations and dismemberment looked upon as proper punishment for the captives. In the painting *The Bodies of Brebeuf and Lallemant Mutilated by the Iroquois*, we can see the main figure leaping around with a head in one hand and an arm in the other, like a cast member from the musical *Sweeney Todd*. Behind this naked sadist, a dismembered leg lies on the ground and a fire burns in the right-hand corner as a reminder that, before long, dinner will be served.

But whatever crime had been committed, no one could merit the appalling conditions Goya depicted in his painting *Interior of a Prison*. Bearing in mind that this was painted from real life, it is horrifying to realize that people were actually kept for years in these circumstances. The picture shows seven prisoners chained and suffering, one naked man lying on the filthy floor with manacles on his ankles and wrists, and a steel collar and chain around his neck. The way these captives were chained meant that movement of the feet was impossible, so that many, too weak to struggle, died where they fell.

Horror fascinated Goya, and he had a

curiosity that encompassed everything — even brutality inflicted on women. *The Beheading* is a terrifying picture of a naked girl, her head jerked back by her executioner as he presses a knife to her throat. Years later, the painter would depict other atrocities, similar in theme to Lucas's *Inquisition Scene*, which shows a variety of prisoners either undergoing, or about to undergo, torture. One man is being turned on a massive wheel studded with razor-sharp spikes that rip at the flesh; others have been crucified; others wait while the priests with their crosses mingle amid the blood.

Appalling conditions like these were a part of Goya's life and were familiar to him, as they were to many painters in France, Italy, and England. Some chose to ignore such cruelty, others to bring it to people's attention. Others continued to work on, impervious, while cities and fortunes crashed around them. There is nothing in the heroic poses of Donatello's fifteenth-century sculptures to suggest that they were created during an uprising in Bologna, when the townspeople, incensed by the massacre of the Bentivoglio family, revenged themselves on the perpetrators by nailing their hearts to the doors of the palace to show their loyalty.

There was also quite a lot of chopping and mutilation taking place when the tranquil Raphael began his career in Perugia; the political climate was so dangerous that few nobles ever lived to collect their bus passes. Indeed, in Mantua, there was an iron cage erected on permanent exhibition. In this was placed a dying man, his appalling agony on view to the townspeople as an example of what they could expect if they got uppity. Yet out of those vicious times came famous collectors and patrons, their influence and wealth securing the best painters and craftsmen in Italy.

One of the most famous figures in the history of art is Lorenzo the Magnificent ('*Il Magnifico Merdo*'), although his career was very nearly ended before it began when traitors (prompted by Pope Sixtus IV) tried to assassinate Lorenzo and his brother at the cathedral in Florence. His brother was killed, but Lorenzo survived to take an appalling revenge on the murderers and gain control of the government. After enduring violent deaths, the assassins' corpses were hung from the windows of their houses as a warning; another traitor was strangled in front of the Ponte Vecchio; and two *priests* were tortured and strangled in public. The act was savage, but Lorenzo knew that he had to get his message across.

Some artists were almost as criminal as their patrons. One such example is Urs Graf, a Swiss engraver, who would work on his creations for a while and then, feeling the need to let off steam, would go and fight as a mercenary. He seemed to relish this dangerous career, and made a great many drawings and paintings of his fellow mercenaries, and of the camp whores, which earned him a reputation as the man with whom one would least like to be seen.

His wife apparently thought the same, and when Graf went off to rape and plunder during the sack of Rome, she waited anxious for news of his return, and then, delighted when it didn't come, presumed her hubby to be dead and dashed off to marry again.

Artists such as Goya and Graf lived amid crime, whereas Cézanne could imagine man's villainous side. Preoccupied as he was with the subject of violence, his work *The Murder* lacks the horror of Goya's beheading scene because Cézanne had not witnessed a murder and Goya had. The Spaniards of the early nineteenth century were surrounded by Satanism, insanity, religious fanaticism, and violence, in a world colored by bullfights and terrorized by the brigands who robbed and murdered women. Goya's scenes are horrible because they are *real*.

Reality continued down the centuries to the First World War, when an artist named George Grosz found himself driven to hatred by the fighting. His real problem was that he could not look at the war dispassionately, and used it as an excuse to loathe mankind in general. His bitterness pours out of his paintings, which include suicides, rapes, and murders, and his picture actually called *The Suicide* shows a dead man in front of a prostitute's house, her half-naked body displayed at the window as she looks out at the cadaver, another corpse hanging from a lamppost.

When the war ended, Grosz still had not worked all the hatred out of his system, and when the Second World War began, he returned to his old themes, only this time he was *living* the horror as he was hunted and pursued across

103

Europe by the Nazis.

Grosz's attitude was not unique. The Victorian Augustus Leopold Egg was much involved with the privations some of his less fortunate contemporaries suffered, and his series of paintings called *Past and Present* depict the decline and fall of a family. Unlike Grosz, Egg relies heavily on sentiment. The story goes as follows: In the first scene, the husband tells his wife that they are broke. She responds with customary British understatement and collapses into a heap on the floor. The next two scenes show her slipping further and further into the mire — her husband dead, her children taken away from her, and then, finally, her own lonely death.

It seems melodramatic now, but at that time, debt was actually regarded as a *crime*. A person falling into debt had no escape; there were no community services. Debt killed, and sent many people to end their lives in the notorious workhouses, or on the streets. Here is another sobering thought: The tale of the woman in *Past and Present* is true.

Velázquez's personality was poles apart from that of Egg or Grosz, and he painted better because of it. This Spaniard let politics, scandal, and intrigue pass him by without so much as an eyebrow raised in acknowledgment, whereas the English painter Thomas Rowlandson relied on crime and folly to provide him with subjects for his caricatures.

Rowlandson began as a serious artist, but success meant money, and money meant temptation, and that led to one inevitable conclusion — gambling. Despite having a rich French aunt who died and left him a huge fortune, Rowlandson's entente cordiale extended only so far, and he soon blew every franc on the cards. Sobered by thoughts of the debtor's jail, Rowlandson considered his future. What was a penniless young man to do, alone in the wilds of wicked London? The answer was obvious — paint it, of course! So for the next few decades, Rowlandson painted every dissolute rake and whore in London, every criminal and bent politician, and every gambler — his paintings providing the money he needed either to gamble with his cronies or to gambol away from his creditors.

Of course, some people prefer animals to people, so the taste for cruelty in animal pictures is particularly disturbing. We already know something about Landseer but who would have thought that the gentle Joseph Wright of Derby was capable of such horrible deeds? This eighteenth-century English painter became famous for his night scenes; virtually everything he painted was so deeply shadowed that his sitters lurched around blindly in a Stygian gloom. Because he painted many scenes of scientific interest, Wright's patrons included the likes of Josiah Wedgwood and Arkwright. Unfortunately, his subjects could sometimes be cruel.

In his painting *An Experiment on a Bird in an Air Pump* in the Tate Gallery, London, we are shown an old, gray-haired professor demonstrating a technique while a white dove is fluttering inside a glass container. Beside him, a little girl looks away, crying. Why? Why indeed. Because our little feathered friend is about to breathe its last and expire — now look at the painting and see whether you still like it.

Death of a different kind colored Bernardino Luini's life. It is difficult to look at his limpid, shadowed Madonnas and think of their creator as a murderer, but, as we have seen already, paintings do not always represent the character of the artist. Luini seems to have had a tiresome life. He worked in Milan and was heavily influenced by Leonardo, and while working on the Pelucca frescoes, he fell in love with Laura, the beautiful daughter of his patron. Unfortunately, her parents did not think Luini was up to much, and thoroughly disapproved of the impoverished artist, especially as Laura had rejected all the suitors they had put forward.

With a cruelty typical of the times, they sent Laura to a nunnery to forget Luini — and presumably anyone else who might catch her fancy. The action broke the painter's heart, and he did not see his love again for many years, until one day he was commissioned to paint some frescoes at the same nunnery where Laura had been sent, and where she remained for the rest of her life.

Disillusioned and bitter, Luini continued with his work and finally fell in love again, this time in Milan. But Venus was not on Luini's side, because the affair was hastily terminated when he *killed* a man in a dispute over his mistress and was forced into the Saronno convent to seek refuge. From then onward, Luini's life is virtually a mystery. We know he worked, but nothing else is recorded about his thoughts or his actions, as he withdrew into himself, a lonely, desolate man.

Niccolò Pizzolo was lonely for other reasons. According to Vasari, this Italian artist wasted his time and his talent by going through the streets picking quarrels instead of getting on with his work. Apparently no one knew whether he was going to shake their hand or ventilate their liver with a rapier. His erratic behavior lost him friends and earned him a great many enemies, but Pizzolo would not listen to advice and continued to go around fully armed, attracting brawls the same way a jam tart attracts wasps. Unfortunately, his lively disposition had frayed too many people's nerves, and for once someone got the boot in first when Pizzolo was ambushed and killed in the street.

Other artists chose to *paint* acts of crime rather than to *live* them. Indeed, the painters surrounded by violence tended to paint delicate, religious themes, and the artists who led quiet lives often painted violence. Turner is a good example of this. After his picture *Snowstorm* was torn apart by reviewers, he continued to work and was championed by Ruskin, but he bore a grudge against the conservative critics and retaliated by painting subjects such as *Slavers Throwing Overboard the Dead and Dying*. This scene illustrates a real event — a cargo of plague-diseased blacks having been abandoned because the insurance company only paid up on people 'lost at sea' and not on the sick.

Of course, there were always artists who loved to paint blood and guts, especially if the blood and guts happened to be spilling all over the canvas. The Italians were superb at this, as the work of Giordano shows, and relished painting-gruesome deaths. One of the nastiest ways to meet your end is to be pulled apart by dogs, especially big ones. This appalling fate befell Jezebel, and was illustrated by Giordano in his painting *The Death of Jezebel*. This fabulously beautiful woman was also vicious and, as the Bible prophesied, she came to a bad end when the King of Israel entered the city of Jezreel and ordered her death.

Mind you, this was not to be any old death — no stabbing or poisoning for this lady. No, sir. Instead, Jezebel was hauled up a tower and then thrown off the top, to be ripped apart by the starving pack of dogs below. Giordano's painting shows the moment she has landed, and the dogs surround her, one dog biting her stomach, another her leg, yet another tearing at her breast, its claws digging into her face as she screams, terrified, writhing on her back.

Jezebel's end was murder, and by all accounts, well deserved. But the *solving* of a murder makes an altogether rarer subject. This situation was depicted by Caracciolo in *The Miracle of St. Anthony of Padua*, a story worthy of Hercule Poirot. Apparently St. Anthony's father was accused of murder and was about to join his victim (due to the ministrations of an angry mob), when St. Anthony stepped in and offered to solve the mystery.

Everyone was agog and they all waited, openmouthed, to hear what he had to say. Unfortunately for St. Anthony and his pa, there had been no witnesses to the crime, and realizing that this was a definite drawback, Anthony promptly revived the murdered corpse and asked for his views on the subject! The obliging cadaver then described what had happened, cleared St. Anthony's father of the murder, and everyone went off quite pleased.

★ ★ ★

The murder of saints has always been a popular subject for artists, and Salome asking for the head of St. John the Baptist probably ranks as one of the most-painted events in the history of art. It's the mixture of sex and violence that appeals to everyone — the lusty young woman dancing for the randy old king, who then has John the Baptist's head lopped off just to please her.

One of the best depictions of this story is Preti's *The Feast of Herod*, in which the head (on the inevitable platter) has just been brought to the table where Salome sits. The most remarkable thing about this painting is the look on her face — there's no trace of repulsion or shame, just the expression someone would use having been offered a stale roll at the Plaza. Rubens's version is much more ghoulish and sickening. His overfed Salome pokes St. John the Baptist in the mouth with a fork as though she were checking to see if he was done enough, while Herod's eyes dart out of his head and a dog claws at his feet to get to the bloody head.

But that, as they say, is all in the past, whereas Reynolds painted a real-life murderer in the person of Guiseppe Baretti, a vain, dapper Italian who came to London to blaze a trail through the literary scene, and ended up famous for other reasons. Apparently, he was self-centered and shortsighted and knifed a pimp to death in a fight, after which he was arrested and only escaped imprisonment due to Reynolds and Johnson, who provided passionate testimonials to his worthiness. The well-known portrait of Baretti shows him peering myopically at a book, and looking very unlikely to have seen anyone smaller than a double-decker bus, let alone stab them accurately enough to kill them. The mystery, unfortunately, died with him.

Crime was a subject beloved of artists, for various reasons. Some lived in criminal times; others lived criminal lives; still others merely painted famous crimes or criminals, their works a living testimony and a record of the murderers who are now dead — the cannibals and brigands Goya painted, Hogarth's Sarah Malcolm, or Reynolds's Baretti. Some even painted themselves, Caravaggio going on record as painting the only known self-portrait of a murderer.

But there is a lighter side to the subject of crime. Goya's life was always a mixture of comedy and tragedy, and something of a surreal element continues to dog his memory. Because he was thought of as such a genius in his day, people wanted to know his secret, and when he died, an eminent phrenologist committed a criminal act and took his *head* away from his body for further examination. It is not recorded what the phrenologist felt, but Goya's head remains at large to this day, and one can only hope that, wherever he is, he doesn't need it.

Artistic Employment

What Would Have Happened If?

What would have happened if Claude Lorraine had kept his job as a pastry cook? Certainly we would have lost a great painter, but, on the other hand, we never would have known what we had missed. His case is not unique; there are many famous painters who began work in jobs they later abandoned to study painting. Others retained their jobs and continued to paint; some were unsuccessful artists and turned to other ways to make a living.

John Herring
was a stagecoach driver who turned to painting horses and other animals. His coach was called the 'High Flyer,' and he worked for Queen Victoria.

Jan van der Heyden
was an artist who, in 1670, started to design fire engines, even writing a book entitled, naturally enough, *The Fire Engine Book*. He then turned to designing street lighting, and became filthy rich.

Vincent van Gogh
wanted to go into the Methodist ministry but was refused admittance, so he took up painting instead.

James Abbott McNeill Whistler
went to West Point Military Academy, but he failed and left to be a painter in London.

Paul Cézanne
was supposed to train to be a lawyer, but he left that profession and began to paint.

Georges Braque
started as an apprentice to a decorator, and then went into fine art.

Honoré Daumier
was first apprenticed to a lawyer, then a book-seller, before discovering his true calling.

Rosa Bonheur
was supposed to start work as a dressmaker, but she persuaded her parents to let her paint instead.

Aelbert Cuyp
Unfortunately, although his work is reaching high prices now, he was not successful in his own lifetime and supplemented his income by working as a brewer.

Camille Pissarro
worked as a clerk in his father's general store before running away to be a painter.

Camille Corot
was forced into business before his father gave him an allowance to study painting.

Claude Vignon
was not content with being a successful painter, book illustrator, and authority on painting; he was also a picture dealer!

William Etty
This marvelous painter of nudes began as an apprentice to a letterpress printer.

Sir Henry Raeburn
was apprenticed to a jeweler before going on to study art.

André Bauchant
was a market gardener until he was forty-six, then he discovered how to paint, and never looked back.

John Constable
began his working life as millhand before taking up painting.

Gustave Courbet
started out studying law and then went into art later.

David Cox
started as blacksmith and was then apprenticed to a locksmith before finally becoming a painter.

Thomas Davie
was a garrison officer in Canada and was *also* a painter.

Max Ernst
was a philosophy student before becoming
a painter.

Paul Gauguin
began as a successful stockbroker before
turning to painting and poverty.

Sawrey Gilpin
became a vicar *after* having been
a painter.

Meindert Hobbema
left painting to take up a position with
the Excise at the age of thirty.

Henry Moore
trained as a teacher before going into
the arts.

Auguste Renoir
started by painting fans for missionaries!

Jusepe de Ribera
began studying for the law, but he rebelled
and ran off to Italy to take up painting.

Henri Rousseau
began as a saxophone player in the 52nd
Infantry band! Then he fought in the
Franco-Prussian War. Then he went into
the Customs service. Lastly, he became
a painter.

Séraphine de Senlis
was a cleaning lady before becoming
a painter.

Dominic Serres
was supposed to enter the Church,
but he ran away to be a painter.

David Smith
was a riveter on a car assembly line before
turning to sculpture.

Willem van de Velde
started as a sailor before turning
to painting.

Alfred Wallis
began his working life as a fisherman, then
began to paint the sea and ships.

Urs Graf
was a Swiss engraver and a mercenary.

Giovanni Santi
worked as a grocer before concentrating on
his painting.

Josef Donoso
was an architect and a painter.

Juan Bautista de Toledo
joined up as a soldier and then changed
his mind and took up painting instead.

Suzanne Valadon
began as an artist's model before turning to
painting.

Armand Guillaumin
worked as a clerk, and dug ditches to finance
his painting.

Henry Fuseli
was forced into becoming a clergyman before
moving on to art as a career.

Frédéric Bazille
should have been a doctor, but he left his
medical studies to become a painter.

Samuel van Hoogstraten
exhausted his capabilities as a painter and then
became a poet and a director of the Dordrecht
mint.

Pietro Torrigiano,
the man who broke Michelangelo's nose, was a
painter *and* a soldier.

4

Patrons

Patrons are lovers of art, people prepared to put their money where their mouths are; people who recognize, appreciate, and pay for skill. These are the unsung heroes, the individuals who support and encourage artists to paint a *Last Supper* or carve a statue such as *David* — which does not mean that they were all jolly good fellows. Some of them were tyrants, some were sexually perverse, and some were just downright odd — like the fabulously wealthy Italian bishop who begged in the streets all day, and at night lay down to sleep on the nearest available pavement.

When artistic patronage was at its height, the Church was the most consistent source of work. Young and hopeful artists vied with each other to catch the eye of the Pope, or the cardinals, whose tastes were either fanatically religious or rabidly erotic. In the potently political atmosphere of Renaissance Italy, Popes had to be politically adept.

So Julius II, who patronized the arts and hired the likes of Raphael and Michelangelo, was well suited to his position, being aggressive, vicious, and indulgent by turns. In nostalgic moods, he liked to brag of his humble beginnings, telling courtiers how he had sold onions when he was a child — a tale that no doubt lost something on the thirtieth time of hearing. Julius II also liked to drink, indulging so often that a wit remarked, ' . . . we only have a Pope until noon, after that, his Holiness is in the Lord's vineyard . . . '

According to a story related by a contemporary, Condivi, if Julius took a fancy to you, you were all right. If he didn't, you had problems. This theory was tested by the young Michelangelo. Because he had been forbidden access to Julius, Michelangelo promptly left town for seven months, in a monumental sulk. But seven months is seven months, after all, and no one can keep it up forever. So after his temper cooled, the artist and the Pope got together again and Julius, not unreasonably, asked why the artist had cleared off in such a fashion.

'Not from ill will, but from disdain,' Michelangelo replied grandly.

A nearby bishop thought this cocky reply was out of order and blurted, 'Pay no attention, Your Holiness, he speaks out of ignorance . . . All artists are like that.'

Julius II did not like to have his audiences interrupted, neither did he like to have anyone telling him what to think. So before the stunned cleric had time to duck, he was treated to an example of the papal clout — in the shape of Julius's fists — as he was beaten out of the room.

The Pope who followed was Leo X, who seems to have been as passive as Julius was hysterical. Although disturbingly bland, he was a mendacious politician who could hold his own with the likes of Erasmus. He was also a gifted musician, but unfortunately he was no oil painting. Grossly fat, he was so shortsighted that he couldn't see anything without the aid of a lens as thick as the bottom of a beer bottle — a drawback that no doubt restricted his artistic appreciation and explains why he preferred his jester's antics to peering into a fog of oil paint.

But these men were all Popes, and that gives a false impression, as not all patrons were ecclesiastical. The Duke of Montague, a famous rake, had no need of religious paintings. His taste turned more to lechery and, to satisfy his impulses, he commissioned Hogarth to paint two erotic pictures — one a scene before seduction, and the other, after seduction. Now Hogarth was no slouch, and he knew that his patron wanted some kind of titillation, an erotic pinup, but he was an artist who painted real life and he gave Montague reality in the *Before Indiscretion* and *After Indiscretion* paintings. Gone is the soft focus, and in its place is truth — the man pulling on his clothes as the woman tries to stop him from leaving, her cap half off her untidy hair, the table beside her turned over in the heat of passion. Montague wanted blatant eroticism, and he got embarrassment and folly instead.

Hogarth would not have tried it on with Cesare Borgia. This notorious second son of Pope Alexander VI began with every advantage, except a good guidance counselor. In an appalling error of judgment, he was entered into the religious life and made a cardinal at the age of fourteen! Regrettably, Cesare was not suited for the job and kept busy fighting, getting taken as a hostage, escaping, and then bumping off his younger brother. Possibly feeling that he had taken a wrong turn in his professional life, Cesare renounced the Church and got married — while he was still sleeping with his sister (who was also sleeping with their father).

Cesare Borgia then became a patron of the arts, and supported many painters, such as Leonardo, when he took time off from poisoning his rivals. But it was a very hazardous business to be hired by Cesare; indeed, a rumor went round that a man had devised a new torture for use in the Borgia dungeon. It was metal, shaped like a bull's head, and fastened over the unfortunate prisoner's head and shoulders. The novelty was that when the tortured man screamed in pain, the noise came out of the head sounding like a bull roaring. Cesare was impressed and ordered the implement to be tried out immediately — on its inventor.

Cesare's other means of murder were quieter, and he became very adept at administering the 'Borgia poison' — a form of food poisoning that struck many a cardinal after a papal feast. However, all good things come to an end, and after the Pope's death, Cesare found himself out on a limb. With grim delight, all his enemies moved in for the kill and murdered him in an ambush — his adored art treasures being stolen and passed on to the next Pope.

Some patrons, such as the Borgias, were fabulously wealthy, but unfortunately such wealth often went hand in hand with a certain nit-picking meanness. Alfonso d'Este, who was the patron of Titian, was somewhat frugal, and

the weekly allowance for the painter reads:
' . . . salad, salt meat, oil, chestnuts, oranges, tallow candles, cheese, and five measures of wine.'

Mind you, Alfonso's patience all but made up for his meanness. With a resignation unusual in Renaissance Italy, he waited *three* years for his *Bacchus and Ariadne*, a painting that he was originally told would take only months to complete. This tardiness on Titian's part did not stop Alfonso's sister, Isabella d'Este, from patronizing the painter. Isabella was a remarkable woman. Clever, ambitious, and well read, she was a witty conversationalist, and played the lute divinely. However, she was also very vain, and when she was in her sixties, she commissioned Titian to paint her in her *twenties*. Even in a dim light at fifty paces, the painting was hardly a truthful likeness, but Isabella was delighted with an artist who could achieve with paint what the mirror could no longer produce.

Many of the wealthiest patrons were much given to vanity and ostentation, and Agostine Chigi was no exception. As a rich sixteenth-century banker, he liked to show off his wealth in extravagant gestures. So at one sumptuous banquet, he had the table cleared by having the hired help toss the gold plates out of the window into the River Tiber. This astonishing display impressed his guests and set tongues wagging — even though every dish had been caught in a net and would be dragged out of the murky depths after the visitors had gone home.

Such gestures only would have annoyed the

Duke of Urbino. Like a good many short men, he had a temper to match his stature, and was notoriously cranky. However, he was very interested in the arts and apparently kind to his wife and servants. But he did not suffer fools gladly and was easily offended, his sword spending more time out of its scabbard than in it. His vicious impatience was no respecter of persons, either, and the Duke is thought to have sent at least one cardinal for a premature chat with his Creator.

At that time in Italy, due to the explosive political situation, there was little safety for even the most powerful, and although the duke had always seemed able to fend for himself, Titian must have been miffed to see another of his patrons bite the dust. As had happened before, a profitable patronage came to a hasty end after a doctored meal. The Duke of Urbino had been poisoned and died in agony a month later.

The rule for survival was simply murder or be murdered, and Ferrante of Aragon, the King of Naples, lived by this creed. He was a wealthy patron, but one for whom no one in his right mind would work. Infamous for his cruelty and savagery, this maniac's riveting personality profile has been left to us by his contemporary Commines. Apparently, when Ferrante wanted to get his revenge on the Signoria of Venice, he didn't take any chances, and instead of simply poisoning his wine, he poisoned every drop of holy water in Venice to get his man.

Ferrante's gruesome reputation was well

earned. All those who got on his bad side were likely to find their heads cut off and *pickled* like gherkins, their bodies preserved and propped up against the walls of Ferrante's gallery with all the other headless cadavers he had amassed for his collection. Apparently, he liked to look at them as he paraded around his works of art.

Other patrons were tame by comparison. George Frederick Watts was a Victorian artist who painted some of the most famous faces in England, such as those of Tennyson, Shrewsbury (who always was trying to save fallen women), and Disraeli. His career was subject to erratic swings of favor, but he certainly benefited from the patronage of Lord and Lady Holland in Florence — even if her interest in him extended beyond his skill with burnt umber.

Queen Henrietta Maria did not fancy van Dyck. This lady was the wife of Charles I and a patron of the arts like her husband. Having seen van Dyck's work, she commissioned him to paint her portrait and waited avidly for the result. Now van Dyck might have looked odd, but he was as sharp as a tack as far as his career went, and knew that a bit of flattery would advance his cause nicely. So he painted the queen not as she was but *as she wanted to be*. The result was a tremendous success with Her Majesty, although Princess Sophia, when she met the queen in person (having only seen the portrait before), was heard to remark, 'It was a surprise to find a little woman with long, lean arms, crooked shoulders, and teeth protruding from her mouth like guns from a fort . . . '

It also helps if your patron is given to grand gestures. When Charles I received his portrait bust from Bernini, he took a ring worth a fortune from his finger and passed it to the messenger, saying, 'Adorn that hand which made so fine a work.'

It goes without saying that Bernini was not a supporter of the English Civil War.

Artists such as Alma-Tadema and Whistler also needed patrons, and Lady Lindsay was a lady who could be relied upon for artistic assistance. Her dinner parties were events at which *contacts* and *contracts* were made. However, if Lady Lindsay was a devoted follower of the arts, her butler was not. Once, when Whistler arrived for dinner dressed casually and sporting the famous gray streak in his dark hair, the butler took one look and then announced him as a guest who had arrived without a tie, and with a feather in his hair!'

The artist Kupecky was literally saved by a patron. His whole life was fraught with difficulties; the son of a poor weaver, he ran away from an unhappy home and went to seek his fortune. Sadly, fortune was not seeking him, and Kupecky soon found himself destitute and begging at a nobleman's house. Luckily for him, he was invited in for a meal instead of being set upon by a German Shepherd.

Now, as luck would have it, the painter Klaus was working on some decorations for the nobleman and Kupecky was fascinated by his work, so fascinated that the artist encouraged him and, when he saw he had talent, took him back to Vienna and helped him to get established. To their mutual delight, Kupecky succeeded. His next patron was King John of Poland, then Emperor Joseph I, and later, Peter the Great. So far, so good.

But into every life a little rain must fall, and before long Kupecky was well and truly drenched. As had happened so many times before, the Inquisition accused Kupecky of heresy. Without stopping to pack, the artist left his influential patrons, and his cushy lifestyle, and fled to Nuremberg.

Patrons could be kind — or they could be peevish. The seventeenth-century French painter Simon Vouet, was already something of a celebrity in his teens and had set up as a portrait painter in England at the advanced age of fourteen. He then traveled constantly, and in good company, until recalled to France by Louis XIII and given a nice little apartment in the Louvre.

Now, as patrons go, Louis XIII was pretty impressive and his support of the painter led to other patrons for Vouet, such as the notorious Cardinal Richelieu. Fame followed, and the artist taught many pupils, and generally made a bundle — until Poussin arrived. The emergence of this dour but talented newcomer prompted Louis XIII to remark peevishly, '*Voilà Vouet bien attrapé!*' Roughly translated, this means 'Here's Vouet's comeuppance!'

It was an unpleasant remark and put Vouet on his guard with his patron, especially as his career died a death and did not recover when Poussin went back home. But at least Vouet had the satisfaction of outliving Louis for six years — God having enforced His own brand of inescapable comeuppance.

Any artist of sensitivity would not have been able to work for a patron such as Khalil Bey. This myopic Turk, who had been Ottoman ambassador in St. Petersburg in the 1850s, collected pornography and chose his artist well, as Gustave Courbet was no prude and was more than able to deal with such patronage. A lover of sex, fêtes, gambling, and collecting women for his harem, Khalil Bey began his patronage of Courbet by buying the artist's notorious *Sleepers*, which depicts two lesbians; The blonde was Whistler's mistress, Jo.

In fact, Courbet was willing to fulfill any of Khalil Bey's erotic requests (he had already achieved a type of erotic infamy with his explicit painting *Woman with White Stockings*) and enthusiastically set about the Turk's new commission for a painting of a woman's genitals. This individual work was kept in a box, the outside of which displayed the kind of scene beloved of the riding set; the inside was for Khalil Bey's shortsighted eyes only.

But at least Khalil Bey paid up on time, an advantage some other painters did not enjoy. Annibale Carracci worked for Cardinal Odoardo Farnese, painting frescoes in the Farnese gallery. For ten years, Carracci worked like a fiend, even taking on other projects for the cardinal — but the cleric would not pay up, or even pay half, and made the artist beg for his wages. In the end, Carracci was exhausted by the constant arguments and slipped into depression, becoming incapable of any work whatsoever. It was said that Farnese's meanness had crippled him mentally and physically.

There wasn't a man made who could cripple Caravaggio more efficiently than he could cripple himself. Yet even this bad-tempered artist managed to win some brownie points from a patron. The Grand Master of the Order of St. John in Malta was so pleased with his commissioned painting that he gave Caravaggio 'a rich collar of gold around his neck, and two Turkish slaves.'

Unfortunately, the Grand Master's good mood didn't last long and when Caravaggio argued with one of the bigwigs in the order he was thrown into prison, with the instruction that he was to be 'deprived of his habit, and expelled and thrust forth like a rotten and fetid limb from our Order and Community.'

With true resourcefulness, Caravaggio escaped and then moved around from place to place, trying to keep one jump ahead of the order and his outraged patron. Having spent too long ogling some schoolboys like an itinerant child molester, Caravaggio was sent packing from Syracuse and returned to Naples. In a valiant attempt to pacify the Grand Master, Caravaggio sent him a painting, *Salome with the Head of the Baptist* — but it had no effect. The Grand Master would be content only if the head in question happened to be Caravaggio's. In a gesture that ranks him among the most ferocious

128

patrons in art history, the Grand Master then sent his henchmen to Naples, where they cornered Caravaggio, slashing his face and throat and leaving him for dead.

5

Art Reviews

It is a well-known fact that artistic criticism is not appreciated. But if criticism from impartial experts is hard to take, it is doubly difficult for artists to swallow criticism from contemporaries.

As a sculptor, Bartolommeo Ammanati was no bungler, as the figure of Neptune in the fountain in the Piazza della Signoria in Florence can testify, but because of his talent he was surrounded by envy. This envy was foolishly put into words by an anonymous rival, who, on seeing the aforementioned Neptune, remarked, '*Ammanati, Ammanati, che bel marmo hai rovinato!*' ('Ammanati, Ammanati, what fine marble you have ruined!')

Needless to say, Ammanati was less than thrilled by this remark, although he was too much of a gentleman to respond at the time. Soon after, however, he married a well-known poet who was more than able to deliver a stinging riposte to any other rivals who went into print — a literary duel, in fact, with insults at ten paces.

William Blake, the artist, writer, and visionary, is now world-famous, despite a singular lack of success in his lifetime, possibly due to the fact that he talked to the dead, and insisted that he held pleasant conversations with a flea. This should not concern us unduly. If Blake wanted to believe that this flea was his agent, he was quite entitled to do so. However, such minor eccentricities are often misunderstood by others, and he found himself quickly at odds with Hayley, the painter, and the engraver Cromek.

Blake's exasperation with them drove him to verse. In a nice twist, he ended up writing a review of *their* work, so the point would be driven home:

A petty, sneaking knave I knew —
Ah, Mr. Cromek, how d'ye do?

Cromek did not see the humor in Blake's little ditty and relationships between them declined rapidly.

No doubt Reynolds failed to see the joke, too, when Blake penned these immortal words about him: 'This man was hired to depress art.' (Insulting the president of the Royal Academy now would not be considered a good move, but then it was comparable to swimming the Channel in concrete boots. In short, Blake's career was *dead*.)

Besides, Reynolds was having troubles of his own, in the unpleasant shape of several dissatisfied customers. He had never been meticulous in his painting techniques and in many pictures the red in the flesh tints faded, so that some of his sitters look like cardiac cases. Walpole was one unhappy customer who suggested that Reynolds should be paid only as long as his paintings lasted, and Walter Blackett did not take his faded portrait in good part, either. Instead, he whipped up a stinging epigram:

Painting of old was surely well designed,
To keep the features of the dead in mind.
But this great rascal has reversed the plan
And made his pictures die before the man.

Complaining had no effect. In fact, an assistant of Reynolds borrowed one of his master's works and was returning it to the studio when, by accident, a passerby bumped into it. The impact unsettled the poorly applied paint and the sitter's hand and most of the face fell off.

Although his critics were apoplectic, Reynolds remained sanguine, and when the Duke of Rutland had cause to complain, the artist merely said that the lumps that had fallen off the painting had done so because of the bumping of the carriage that had transported it. When the painting was hung on the wall, there would be no further deterioration, he assured the aristocrat. (God help anyone who happened to knock into it; no doubt they would have been buried under several feet of Naples yellow.) Lord Holderness didn't fare too well, either — a few years after his portrait was painted, his forehead began to peel off.

It is an accepted belief that anything new in art is no good. Even so, the vitriol that greeted certain works was truly astounding. The Members of the PRB (the initials standing for the Pre-Raphaelite Brotherhood) were deluged with the kind of reviews that can burn the ink off a newspaper. The *Times* said of Millais's *Christ in the House of His Parents*, 'the picture is plainly revolting' and the *Literary Gazette* called it 'a nameless atrocity.' Apparently, they didn't like it.

But their response is tame compared with the poison that poured out of Charles Dickens' pen. On seeing *Christ in the House of His Parents*, he wrote:

> In the foreground ... is a hideous, wry-necked, blubbering, red-haired boy in a nightgown ... for the contemplation of a kneeling woman, so horrible in her ugliness that (supposing it were possible for any human to exist for a moment with that dislocated throat) she would stand out from the rest of the company as a monster in the vilest cabaret in France or the lowest gin-house in England.

His words made the artist burn with rage for a long time, until an uneasy friendship grew between them. The last word, however, did *not* go to the writer, and Millais's drawing of Dickens on his deathbed was the final act of revenge.

In France, Manet was similarly thrashed. When his *Déjeuner sur l'herbe* was exhibited, it caused enough of a scandal to force the closure of the exhibition, and his *Olympia* fared no better when the critic Amédée Canteloube set eyes upon it: 'Nothing so cynical has ever been seen as this *Olympia*, a sort of female gorilla ...

Truly, young girls and women about to become mothers would do well, if they are wise, to run away from this spectacle.'

Eleven years later, Manet was brave enough to try again and exhibited his picture, *The Laundress*.

Le Figaro said of it: 'This is flat; it is not modeled. It looks like the Queen of Spades from a set of playing cards, rising from her bath.'

Gustave Courbet was another to feel the cold draft of disapproval. When he showed one of his gigantic nudes, Napoleon III struck the painting with his walking stick, offended by its realism. The same realism sometimes restricted Courbet's imagination. When he was asked to paint some angels for a church picture, he replied, 'Show me an angel, and I will paint one. I have never seen an angel.'

After leading a highly charged and disruptive life, it is doubtful whether he ever did.

Perhaps the best way of avoiding criticism is to fire the first shot. William Aikman, the Scottish portrait painter, moved to London after Geoffrey Kneller's death to make a killing. Picking up the deceased's trade, he quickly moved up the ranks and became friends with Swift and the waspish, four-foot-six Alexander Pope. But being friendly with Pope did not mean that you were exempted from a savage art review, and, possibly in an attempt to get the boot in first, Aikman penned these lines on his portrait of Allan Ramsay.

Here painted on this canvas clout
By Aikman's hand is Ramsay's snout.

Pope thought it was an amusing remark, but Ramsay didn't, and struck back by making the painter wait for payment.

Naturally, there was always sniping between painters. Most artists cannot resist taking a swipe at someone else's work, and the congenial John Constable certainly couldn't resist the temptation when defeated in the Royal Academy election by William Etty (the painter of nudes). He was not at all magnanimous in defeat and, looking at Etty's superbly painted posteriors, commented noisily on 'Etty's bumboat' and his 'shaggy posteriors of satyrs.' Etty, the son of a miller ('Like Rembrandt,' as he used to say grandly), did not stoop to respond and remained smugly aloof.

To be criticized by a rival is hard, but to have your faults pointed out by the very man who taught you must be agony. At least, that was how Reynolds must have found it. Having spent considerable time abroad and having been influenced by his study of Rembrandt, Reynolds was complimenting himself on his new approach when he was visited by his old master, Hudson. After scrutinizing his pupil's new work, Hudson remarked, 'By God, Reynolds, you don't paint like you used to.'

The recipient's reply is unreported, although it is to be hoped that he turned a deaf ear.

The Victorian painter G. F. Watts hit a sticky patch, too, when his painting *Life Illusions* was torn to shreds by a critic in *The London Quarterly Review*, who objected to such things as 'the aged angel who is so absorbed in his book

135

that the next step will take him over the edge of the precipice' and 'a knight, of mature years, riding madly in a very confined space, after a soap bubble.'

An unknown artist expects vitriolic reviews; a well-established painter does not. So when Horace Walpole saw Hogarth's depiction of *Sigismonda*, the artist was infuriated to read the following criticism: 'a maudlin whore tearing off the trinkets that her keeper had given her . . . her fingers are bloody . . . as if she had just bought a sheep's pluck from St. James's market . . . '

Hogarth took the review with all the grace of a demented bull, as the model who had been torn limb from limb was actually his wife. Perhaps he was also hurt that Walpole did not realize the great length to which he had gone in the pursuit of reality. The heart over which Sigismonda grieves was actually painted from life; his friend, the surgeon Sir Caesar Hawkins, had provided a suitable organ. Unfortunately, the effect is somewhat strained, as the heart has more life than the model, and seems about to burst over the rim of the goblet like a blood-soaked Christmas pudding.

Hogarth was not an artist to let every spiteful review go by unrewarded. On the contrary, he was a man who enjoyed a good grudge and when he quarreled with the poet Charles Churchill, who had written a satire on his work, the artist passed his own critical judgment by doing a painting of his dog urinating all over Churchill's essay.

Even when he was powerful and rich, John

Millais still suffered from the spite of the critics, and his painting *The Eve of St. Agnes* met a very hostile reception in some quarters. The picture shows a woman standing in the moonlight, white light falling across her body, the window frame making a pattern of shadow on the floor. Ethereal and moody as it was, some critics did not consider such effects romantic. 'I can't bear that woman with the grid iron,' blustered an unimpressed Sir Francis Grant.

Théodore Géricault was overfond of the harsh realities of life — dissections, asylums, and the like — whereas his contemporary Ingres was more concerned with nude women. So when Géricault's works were exhibited, Ingres had quite a lot to say on the subject: 'I should like to see removed from the Louvre that picture of the *Medusa* and those two big Dragoons ... I should like to have them placed in some corner of the Navy Department; then they will no longer corrupt ... the public ... I resent pictures of the dissecting room; they show us man only as a cadaver ... ' And so he went on, and on.

Poor Géricault had few champions; even his teachers advised him to give up painting, and his insistence on illustrating subjects such as *The Inquisition* and *The Slave Trade* offended many. Speaking of the notorious *The Raft of the Medusa*, C. P. Landon wrote, ' ... what public building, what royal palace or collector's gallery would be willing to house this painting? ... Once he has learned to control his brush and turn it in a more fitting direction he will profit considerably . . . '

The only remark one can make after reading that is that we all know about Géricault, but who was C. P. Landon?

In general, many French painters came in for some rough criticism, and sometimes from unexpected quarters. Emile Zola, of *J'Accuse* fame, was not above j'accusing a painter of sentimental romanticism, and said of the work of the gentle Corot: 'If Corot would consent to kill once and for all the nymphs with whom he populates his woods and replace them with pleasant women, I would like him beyond measure.'

But Corot stuck to his nymphs and Delacroix stuck to *his* romantic visions, although it didn't do him much good. Just read Gautier's perfect example of the art of damning with faint praise: 'Delacroix has pale olive skin, rich black hair . . . People found he resembled Lord Byron . . . Nobody was more seductive than he . . . Too bad that such a charming man paints in such an atrocious manner . . . '

Even the public joined forces in condemning him. His painting, *Liberty Leading the People*, depicts a voluptuous, half-naked, rabble-rousing female inciting her followers to fight and kill for freedom. When it was exhibited, one critic, Heinrich Heine, reported a conversation he had overheard when a father tried to explain the painting to his daughter.

'She is a goddess of liberty.'

'But, Daddy, she does not even wear a chemise!'

'A true goddess of freedom, my dear child, seldom has a chemise and is therefore very angry at all the people who wear clean linen.'

Gustave Courbet's painting *Return from the Conference* was a failure. Most people loathed it. The official Salon thought it was an obscenity and refused to hang the picture, and even the Salon des Refusés (which specialized in hanging the works no other place would hang) declined ungraciously. In fact, it was criticized to such an extent that Courbet must have been stunned when it was finally sold. Unfortunately, the buyer turned out to be a fervent Catholic, who, after obtaining the picture, passed his own critical judgment and consigned it to the flames.

At the same time, back in England, Turner was suffering for his art. The painting *Snowstorm* was exhibited after the artist had been strapped to the mast for hours in the middle of a tremendous storm at sea. His reason for this singular behavior was that he wanted to watch the elements in all their frenzy, so that he could reproduce them faithfully on canvas later. One has to bear in mind that this was not only a brave thing to do but also that Turner was sixty-six years old at the time.

Of all his paintings, maybe this one was the greatest labor of love; when it was exhibited, the peevish reviews shattered Turner. His majestic storm was seen as 'all soapsuds and whitewash.'

But occasionally even criticism can be amusing — when viewed with hindsight. One might have thought that Michelangelo would escape censure — not so. While he was putting the finishing touches to his statue *David*, a prelate came by and glanced up at the magnificent work. Irritated, Michelangelo continued and ignored him. The clergyman stared, coughed, and finally asked the sculptor whether he did not think the nose of *David* was too big.

Taking in a deep breath, Michelangelo picked up some loose chippings from the statue (without the prelate noticing) and then pretended to work away at the nose of *David*, letting the chippings filter through his hand at the same time. After another moment, Michelangelo paused, and then asked the cleric whether the statue looked better now.

'Oh much,' the man replied blindly, 'much, much better.'

The Blunders

Now and again, the artist makes a real mistake. Perhaps it's due to an oversight, or maybe it's just a blunder, but here are a few little gems.

- Brueghel's man with three legs in the painting *Peasant Wedding*. (He is one of the two carrying the tray.)
- What about the etching by Rembrandt of the couple making love? Look closely: The woman has three hands.
- Rembrandt came a cropper with his drawing of the Virgin and Child suspended on clouds; if you turn the sketch upside down and you can see another head popping out of the cloud.
- There is a strange metamorphosis taking place in Goya's painting of *Isabel Lobo de Porcel*. Apparently the lady is changing sex, because she is certainly developing a lovely black mustache. This facial hair actually comes from the painting of a man underneath, which is bleeding through.
- There is a splendid example of early puberty in Zurbarán's painting *The Adoration of the Shepherds*. Just look at the cherub at the top of the canvas with its black mustache!
- Who owns the hand in the background, far left, of the painting *The Fortune Teller* by Georges de la Tour? Is it the woman with the

white sleeve, or the brunette behind?

- Speaking of the Georges de La Tour painting, who wrote the word *merde* (shit) on the woman's white collar on the far left?
- One of my favorites has to be Millais's *The Woodman's Daughter* (Guildhall art gallery). This picture shows us a boy holding out strawberries to the woodman's daughter of the title. Now, apart from the fact that the girl's feet are rapidly becoming transparent, the boy's extended right arm is nine inches shorter than his left. However, if it had been painted at the same length as his other one, his reach would have been longer than Paul Bunyan's and his outstretched arm would have socked the woodman's daughter squarely on the jaw.

6

Illness and Deformity

In the twentieth century, we think that we are more civilized than preceding generations that reveled in the depiction of illness and deformity. However, if the truth be known, most people still have a ghoulish fascination with the macabre, and many paintings leave a trail of clues on the canvas, pointing to a variety of illnesses.

In Hogarth's work, the signs of smallpox are obvious, as are the symptoms of rickets. In the time of Velázquez, when venereal disease was rife in the courts, victims were allocated a permanent nurse, usually a nun. Syphilis passed on to a child in the womb was recognized almost at birth, the infant possessing the peculiar 'saddle nose' of the disease, as seen in the figure in the right-hand background of the painting *Las Meninas*.

Because of the formidable amount of inbreeding, especially in royal circles, weaknesses were exaggerated almost to the proportions of a caricature. A prime example may be seen in the portrait of Carlos the Bewitched of Spain, who had the severely undershot jaw and weak eyes of the Royal House, and a liver that, on autopsy, was found to be 'the size of a walnut.'

Deformity, to some jaded palates, has always had novelty value. Indeed, most European courts kept dwarfs, many of whom were painted, either with their royal patrons or alone. Velázquez painted a small hydrocephalic child and Veronese used several adult male dwarfs in his massive religious paintings.

Illness or deformity in the painter himself was also found to be fascinating, a well-known example being Toulouse-Lautrec. Other artists, such as Diaz de la Pẽna, found celebrity due to infirmity. He had his leg removed as a young man and his career benefited enormously afterward as a result of this. Unfortunately, this particular painter was doomed: His artistic career was cut short by the bite of a startled viper.

Illness was considered to be a fascinating topic for a painting, and many artists achieved their notoriety with peculiar subjects. Holman Hunt, the Victorian artist, was much affected by the battlefield of Balaclava, which was still scattered with the bones of the dead when he saw it. His painting *The Sleeping City* is a monument to those fallen heroes, and a worthy subject. Would that Holman Hunt had always been so reverential of life.

The theme of his painting *The Scapegoat* comes from the Jewish practice of laying the sins of the people on a goat allowed to escape to the wilds to perish along with the sins. It gives some insight into this misguided painter to learn that he chose such a horrible subject to paint, but his inhumanity was more than equal to the Jewish animal lover's when he began to paint in the arid, scorched wasteland by the Dead Sea.

Working in intense heat, with little regard for the goat's welfare, the disorientated Holman Hunt continued painting until the unfortunate animal expired. (It is only a rumor that he then ate it.) However, what is known for a fact is that, with true Victorian callousness, he bought another goat and continued to paint what is probably the most hideous and macabre work ever to have stained a canvas.

Baron Antoine-Jean Gros was another artist who liked to tackle the seamier side of life. His career began well and, after he had been taught by David, he left for Italy at the beginning of the Reign of Terror, and was then recommended to Napoleon by the worthy Josephine. Later, Gros became a war artist for Napoleon, and like a nineteenth-century Saatchi and Saatchi, fueled the fires of the political myth. An adept politician in his own right, Gros rode the changes in rule well, and was made official painter to Louis XVIII. Unfortunately, he had a rotten marriage and was subject to depression, so that later, when his classical works were ridiculed, he went into a decline and threw himself into the Seine to drown.

However, back to his heyday: While Gros was happy working with the stunted emperor, he produced some remarkable work, including the *Pesthouse at Java*. This painting was something of a publicity ploy, as the British soldiers had besmirched Napoleon's reputation by announcing that he had deserted his plague-sick men because they slowed his retreat. Controversy raged, and even while Gros was painting

145

Napoleon bringing comfort to his sick men in the pesthouse, an onlooker was reporting that the emperor halfheartedly kicked the infected men with the toe of his boot.

Aside from the plague, other illnesses caught the eye of artists; warts obviously held a fascination for Ghirlandaio, as can be seen in his painting *Francesco Sassetti with His Grandson*. This portrait is unremarkable in composition but riveting in its physical detail; the old man leaning toward his young visitor appears to have half a cauliflower stuck on his nose. Scars and warts are always good material for artists, and Oliver Cromwell endeared himself mightily when he instructed the artist to paint him 'warts and all.'

Van Dyck was also a great admirer of scar tissue and went to town on Henry Danvers, Earl of Danby, who appears to be sporting a sea slug under his left eye. Giordano differed in that he favored sores, and painted them frequently, as in the work *St. Tommaso da Villanova Distributing Alms*. The beggar at the front has his legs covered in ulcers and bloody sores, the flesh darkening around the open wounds.

The little girl in a painting by Metsu, *The Sick Child*, doesn't look too healthy, either, her pale face drawn and old for her years, and her condition hinting at more than a childhood ailment. And what about Jan Sanders van Hemessen's painting, *The Surgeon*? This surely satisfies anyone's appetite for the grotesque. In the Netherlands, surgery was carried out in the city square, and this operation involved the strapping down of the patient in a chair, followed by the diagnosis of feeble-mindedness caused by a stone in the head. (Ergo, the happy American phrase 'rocks in the head.')

Any charlatan could convince the gullible, and by means of a simple trick the quack would make a cut in the patient's forehead and, with a little sleight of hand, produce the stone that had caused all the trouble. Naturally, he charged for his services, so that the poor patient and his family returned home a lot poorer and certainly no wiser.

Infestation by head lice, although it doesn't really count as illness, crops up so many times in Dutch art that it deserves a mention. Many a picture was given a sentimental title such as *Mother Combing a Child's Hair*, until it was discovered that the parent was actually searching for lice.

The Dutch always had a liking for paintings of doctors and quacks because these people were so much a part of their lives, and they also had a special fondness for 'lovesickness,' which was apparently diagnosed by a quick pulse and a red urine sample. Such novel means of diagnosis extended to pregnancy as well, the quack detecting its signs by burning a ribbon in a brazier. In Schalcken's picture *The Visit to the Doctor*, the quack holds up a lurid urine sample and the patient weeps. (Whether that was due to the diagnosis, or the fee, we aren't told.) This amorous illness was not always the complaint, however, and in Dou's painting of the same subject, *The Doctor's Visit*, the old lady has just been given the sentence of death.

On the bleak side, there are some powerfully moving accounts of illness throughout art. Rembrandt's drawing of his dying wife, Saskia, is as tender as his sketch of the crippled beggars who roamed the countryside, and the pitiful drawing of his dead baby son. Poverty fascinated him, and he did many etchings of the beggars who tried to make a living on the streets, either alone or with their starving dogs. He also etched scenes of blindness, crippled old age, and obesity.

Rembrandt wasn't the only one to find fat intriguing. Bartholomeus van der Helst's painting *Gerard Andriesz Bicker* presents us with a gigantic, smug, overstuffed youth, wearing what appears to be half of a curtain around his impressive girth. Despite the artist's best efforts to make the sitter look attractive, he still looks like a fat boy in fancy dress, and a certain candidate for heart failure.

Adriaen Brouwer didn't feel the need to glamorize anything. He painted what he saw, so when he saw the grubbier side of life, he painted that. His picture *A Village Doctor Bandaging a Peasant's Arm*, gives us a crude idea of the standard of medicine available to the seventeenth-century Dutch (and makes us marvel that there are any twentieth-century Dutch). The doctor, who looks three sheets to the wind, is bandaging an injury with dark gray cloth, his lips pursed with the effort, the patient wincing at his fierce administrations. Just to further aggravate matters, there is a hooded onlooker peering into the wound like a medical voyeur.

However, this constant interest in blood and guts only becomes comprehensible when a miraculous transformation takes place and gruesome scenes become works of art. The painting *The Anatomy Lesson of Dr. Tulp* by Rembrandt is wonderful, but it is still a picture of a corpse with its left arm skinned, its veins being plucked like the strings of a Welsh harp. The anatomy theatre, in Amsterdam, where this scene is said to have taken place, was built at Tulp's bidding, and people actually *paid* to go to see a corpse being dissected. (The show began with disembowelling and then presumably continued as long as there were any members of the audience still conscious.) Apparently most of the cadavers were criminals, or those poor souls who had no family to object to their relation being carved up like a third-rate variety-club act.

Rembrandt's later work *The Anatomy Lesson of Dr. Joan Deyman* differs from his earlier work in that only a fragment of the painting exists — but what a fragment! Here we have a cadaver facing the onlooker full on, its stomach emptied, the huge cavity grinning open, while the man's scalp has been neatly parted down the middle like the hair of a Victorian gentleman, the brain exposed like a lurid sponge. One can only wonder *who* the body was, before it was so unceremoniously hacked up — it certainly wasn't one of those sitters who paid Rembrandt fortunes to have their likenesses struck. This gentleman must have been the artist's best sitter;

after all, he was in no condition to argue if he thought it was a bad likeness.

Thomas Eakins, an American painter, was similarly fascinated by surgery. His famous painting of *The Gross Clinic* shows the surgeon demonstrating his skills in front of a packed house of medical students, the only note of melodrama creeping in with the wife who sits, off center, with one arm over her face to block out the view.

Sometimes artists inserted very personal and very gruesome details into their paintings, like Michelangelo in the *Last Judgment*, who painted his own features on the face of the flayed figure of St. Bartholomew. Caravaggio was also attracted to the grim self-portrait and in his *David with the Head of Goliath* his features are those of the fallen giant.

Other painters did not go to such masochistic lengths, and preferred inflicting punishment on others. Rembrandt painted the horrendous *The Blinding of Samson* with such relish that the pike being forced into Samson's eye causes the blood to spurt out in a mass of gore. Further examination reveals other horrors, such as the fierce pulling of Samson's beard to hold his head still, and the sharpened blade approaching his other eye. The whole painting is repellent and it is not at all surprising that the receiver of this doubtful gift declined it graciously and sent it back to the puzzled painter with indecent haste.

Possibly due to the nature of artists, the fierce rivalry, and the impossible demands of patrons, many painters ended their lives in a state of insanity. Even art critics were not immune, for example, the notable John Ruskin leaving this world with fewer brains than he came in with. His life was a privileged one that should have been blessed, but after his doomed marriage and his outraged attack on Whistler, he was soon on the ropes. Years of high moral stands and attacks on industrialism followed and, although his art criticism was meticulous and often inspired, he died mad.

Hugo van der Goes went the same way. As possibly the most gifted early Netherlandish painter, he had a considerable reputation in his own time and was deservedly famous. Then things began to go wrong for him. Around 1480, Hugo joined his brother in an Augustinian monastery near Brussels, where he continued to paint and receive important patrons. Hugo then decided that a holiday would be nice and set off to Cologne, but he never made it and was taken ill on the journey. From then on, Hugo slipped downhill into religious melancholia, and then insanity, a condition in which he died.

Landseer's first breakdown occurred, as we know, after a disappointment in love. Shattered that he had been given the elbow, his mental state became unhinged and from then on his life was punctuated by strange aberrations in behavior. In the end, a contemporary described him as 'a dangerous homicidal maniac,' and Queen Victoria added her own diagnosis when she said that Landseer was 'hardly fit to be about, and looked quite dreadful.'

In his last years, Landseer was looked after by

Mrs. Pritchard, a thin, wizened old lady whom the artist called his 'Pocket Venus,' much to the astonishment of onlookers who saw a woman more like a garden gnome than a goddess. Yet Mrs. P. had the artist's interests at heart and controlled his insanity with kindness, refusing any salary. As the madness progressed, Landseer's mind could jam like some kind of freeze-frame mechanism, and on one occasion he kept muttering, 'Bulls, bulls' (it was definitely 'bulls') 'bulls, bulls,' and then drew everything with that name: bulrush, bull-frog . . .

A visit from Landseer could be dangerous, too. One old lady, being a good friend and feeling sorry for the painter, received him when she had bronchitis. The artist came in, looked around, and then sat down on her chest. Being a large man, he soon caused some obstruction in the unfortunate woman's breathing, and only the prompt intervention of the diminutive Mrs. P. prevented the invalid's early arrival at the Pearly Gates.

But at least Landseer was treated with kindness, something sadly unavailable in eighteenth-century London. As we can see in the last painting of Hogarth's *The Rake's Progress*, the mad were treated like animals, and were locked away in cells in conditions of freezing cold, with no sanitation, shackled to the walls by chains, sometimes with their arms clamped down to their sides like criminals. There they were left in their own excreta. Often their heads were shaved because it was thought 'to cool the brain,' and they were stripped or kept in cages, where they could not stand up.

As a further cruelty, enemas were administered to calm them down, and some unfortunates were plunged into alternate hot and cold baths to quiet them.

Madness was not treated with sympathy; in fact, it was thought of as disgusting or amusing, and the rich, both men and women, came to places such as Bedlam, a famous asylum, to watch the inmates perform. Some people even arranged visits there as a diversion at the end of an evening spent playing cards. One character in the Bedlam scene of Hogarth's *The Rake's Progress* is so deluded that he thinks he is a king, and sits naked with a regal expression on his face — although he happened to be unregally emptying his bowels at the time.

Hogarth was sympathetic to lunatics, but he had a merciless eye for quacks, and depicted many of these real-life crooks who made a living from plying fake cures or abortions. A wonderful example of this type of charlatan is recorded forever in *The Rake's Progress*. The quack, whom the rake and his child-mistress visit, was actually a man named Dr. Misaubin, who was notorious in London. It is not certain whether Hogarth painted his real consulting room, but the weird objets d'art are very revealing. If you look at the picture closely, you can make out an embalmed body in the cupboard, a painting of a hermaphrodite, a man with his head between his shoulders, and what appears to be a sexually active skeleton.

These quacks were often assisted by a 'nurse,' who was usually a procuress or an abortionist, and although they made a repulsive couple, the social conditions of the time were so appalling that many pregnancies were terminated by these types in the most brutal ways. Even if the child *did* live long enough to draw breath, its life was often short, and indeed there were many accounts of babies left abandoned on the roadsides — either murdered at birth or left exposed to the elements or the animals.

In some paintings, the signs of illness are obvious, but in others there are clues to point to the *results* or *aftermath* of disease. In a number of well-known pictures, wigs cover bald heads (a result of mercury treatment for the pox) and, in severe cases, face masks were employed, as shown in the works of Pietro Longhi. In Hogarth's day, syphilis was an occupational hazard for the prostitutes and the telltale black beauty patches covered the first signs — sores — but as the illness progressed, more drastic symptoms showed. The maid in *The Harlot's Progress* has lost her nose to the disease.

The doctors then were powerless to halt the infection and relied on hopeless treatments such as 'salivation'; patients were given mercury pills to make them salivate, which the quacks thought was a treatment by which the body rid itself of VD. Other cures included wrapping patients in many layers of clothing and forcing them to sweat, which was another way it was believed the infection could be expelled, or making the patient wear an anodyne necklace. None of these actions had any effect — except that the mercury caused the patients' teeth and hair to fall out.

Children who inherited VD showed the signs in childhood, as can be seen in the last painting of Hogarth's *The Harlot's Progress*, where the whore's son is already wearing black patches on his face and a brace on his leg to correct the rickets, a symptom of hereditary syphilis. Hogarth didn't just concentrate on the symptoms of VD, though; his other paintings show a man having an attack of the gravel in *An Election Entertainment*, a girl dabbing at a sore on her mouth in *The Rake's Progress*, and a man having a fit while he is being bled in *An Election Entertainment*.

Other painters preferred to work on the onlooker's senses. Fromentin, one of the so-called Orientalists, painted a harrowing picture called the *Land of Thirst*, a view that is guaranteed to make anyone reach for the gin and tonic. Nineteenth-century taste relished what were called 'disaster paintings,' in the same way that we watch interminable movies where Charles Bronson saves people by the dozen.

The same taste demanded sensationalism in the salon, and this was provided by the likes of Fromentin, who wrote travel books, which, had they ever reached the general public, would have stopped the tourist trade overnight. He also painted lurid pictures of men dying of thirst to accompany his literary descriptions of a heat 'which bored through your skull like a corkscrew.'

Géricault was not interested in the desert or the heat — his curiosity turned to a study of madness and he painted ten portraits of the inmates of a Paris asylum, thinking, as many did then, that a person's face showed his or her character and any tendency toward criminality. Géricault's curiosity was insatiable, and before long he was making drawings of nudes being tortured, and of dismembered heads and limbs, even going to hospitals and studying the faces of patients in extremis, and looking at newly dead corpses 'which he procured from the neighboring hospital and the morgue: . . . his atelier began to look like a slaughterhouse.'

Fascinated, he trailed round the streets, too; 'he listened to the desperate and watched the deranged wherever he could find them.' And there were always his acquaintances: 'To a friend whose face was transformed because he was suffering from jaundice, the artist exclaimed, 'How beautiful you are!' and hastened to fetch his paint box.'

Géricault became so intrigued with the dead that he began to take his work home with him, and nightly the odd head or arm would leave the morgue and end up in the studio. To really get a feel for the scene, remember that Géricault also *slept* in that room, while the various human remains watched over him. Now, you would think that this would be ghoulish enough for anyone, but not Géricault. Not content with drawing dismembered bodies and heads, he decided to keep them and make studies of the flesh decomposing — all in the name of art, of course.

The Italians liked to paint illness and injury, too, as you can see from looking at Traversi's

Wounded Man, a painting that shows us a young man baring his side to the bemused attention of a bewigged quack. The only thing keeping the man's mind off his agony is the young woman in the low-cut dress, who is cradling his head and tickling him under his chin at the same time. The whole scene is painted with considerable relish, the onlookers fading into the dark background, while the man's side is illuminated like Madison Square Garden.

The gods didn't fare too well when it came to illness, either — one need only look at Argus, with his head cut off, and Rubens's painting of Prometheus's liver being torn out by an eagle. Apparently this was his punishment for stealing fire from the gods, and although it seems horrible enough, the liver isn't torn out once, but repeatedly, as the liver regrows and the bird comes back for a second course.

To continue the theme of sexuality and injury, think of St. Sebastian, who was shot with arrows; of St. Agatha, who had her breasts torn off; St. Apollonia, who had her teeth pulled out; and St. Lucy, who had her throat slit. Other tortures unconcerned with sexuality include those of St. James the Less, who was clubbed to death with a fuller's staff, and of St. Laurence, who was roasted on a gridiron like a giant waffle.

It is not surprising to hear that Caravaggio painted deformity, but it is surprising to discover that he painted it so seldom. However, his favorite model, who sat for *St. Catherine of Alexandria* did have a deformed third finger on her left hand. It is very easy to spot in some paintings of her; in others, Caravaggio has propped up the deformed digit on a handy piece of furniture. In the *St. Catherine*, it is obvious, and, unsupported, hangs below her little finger, although in the *Sts. Martha and Mary Magdalene* in the Christ Church Library, Oxford, it is held up by a conveniently placed mirror.

Tooth pulling has been recorded on canvas, too. In seventeenth-century Holland, it was not the private act it is now, and the dentist was usually another wandering quack who would set up his stall and treat people in the market square. Jan Victors's painting *The Dentist*, shows the quack pulling out an offending tooth while the patient grips his tunic in agony. Gerrit Dou's *Quack* is another painting that displays these wandering charlatans, who traveled the countryside treating the gullible before moving on again. Not that all the onlookers were simple idiots; in Dou's painting *The Tooth Puller*, we can spot Rembrandt's father watching the event avidly.

The Foot Operation by Isaack Koedijck depicts a less common subject for a painting. The patient in this has just had an operation on his foot, and sits with his leg stretched out as the young barber-surgeon bandages the wound. On the floor, there is a smattering of blood to prove that surgery had taken place and that this was not quackery — like the 'stones in the head' ploy, or the *kopsters*' treatment, which consisted of putting hot metal cups on the patient to 'pull out' the sickness. No, this foot operation is real and has been held in a respectable establishment, even if it is a far cry from Park Avenue.

The room has all the attributes that would have existed in a Dutch consulting room then: The human skull (possibly from a not-too-well-satisfied customer), the urine bottles, and the crocodile without which no surgery is complete. In fact, the patient in this picture manages to look reasonably satisfied with his treatment, even if his cockerel has keeled over at his feet.

Illness was not restricted to the lower classes. If you look at Mantegna's *Camera degli sposi* (or *The Court*), you can see what many medical men have detected as signs of rickets in the rich Gonzago children. The portrait of the young woman in the work *Too Late* in the Tate Gallery, London, shows her leaning on a stick and about to succumb to tuberculosis, her unfaithful lover returning too late. Sickness was greatly beloved of the Victorians, which explains why the legend grew around Elizabeth Barrett before she rose from her sickbed and ran off with the dashing Browning.

Many an artist has made his name on the strength of a good sentimental painting, and Sir Luke Fildes was no exception. This artist's most famous work is *The Doctor*, which depicts a dying child in a poor home, the good doctor watching over him as his parents wait for the end. This tragic story was true. The artist's first child had died while he was an infant, having been tended by a doctor not unlike the one in the painting. It is a memorial to the physician and to the child.

Edvard Munch's *Sick Girl* is not romantic at all. Here we have a very poorly looking individual, sitting up in bed with her hair everywhere, and her mother weeping on the pillow beside her. Yet the model for this was Munch's sister, Sofie, who died from tuberculosis when she was in her teens, and the painting has a despair and anger completely alien to the sentimentality of Fildes's.

Although they generally had little hesitation in painting other people suffering, not many artists would be prepared to show *themselves* in bed looking as sick as a parrot, but Goya was game for anything. *Goya and Dr. Arrieta* shows the deaf artist clutching his bedclothes while the doctor tries to get some medicine down his reluctant throat. It should come as no surprise to learn that Goya made a slow recovery, especially as it was probably hindered by what appears to be an audience of death masks behind his bed.

Religious paintings can provide quite a few nasty shocks, too. In Carpaccio's *Burial of Christ*, Jesus is laid out on a hard bench in a desolate place, skeletons and corpses in different degrees of decay arrayed behind him. On His left is half a torso and a dismembered arm, and on His right, in the far background, a gray cadaver stands like an emaciated beggar with a pile of skulls at his feet.

The medical appliances previous generations used to aid their recovery are also intriguing. In Moroni's portrait *Il Cavaliere del Piede* ('Bigshot with Bad Foot'), there is a splendid example of the basic medical prosthesis available in

160

sixteenth-century Venice. Apparently this gentleman's left foot did not work in tune with his right, and so, to prevent him falling over, a curious metal strap was placed under the instep of the offending foot and then another was tied around the knee, a crude metal splint running between the two joints. It looks uncomfortable and unreliable. One wrong step and the cavalier would be stabbed in the gut by a flying crutch.

The story of Lazarus rising from the dead is popular, but it is usually romanticized, and only the fifteenth-century French artist Nicolas Froment, shows us how it really might have been. In his painting, we see Lazarus rising up, a ghastly green-gray color, while one onlooker reels back in shock and two others cover their noses to block out the smell of rotting flesh.

Incidences of *accidental* deformity are not as well known, although the painting of *Cardinal Richelieu* by Philippe de Champaigne deserves to be. Going on the usual artistic belief that the head is a tenth the size of the body, Richelieu's appearance must have been remarkable, as he must have been close to eight feet tall — a fact never mentioned in history books. Van Dyck inflicted the same kind of deformity on the Marchesa Brignole Sale. This lady is sitting down, and probably with good reason — if she had stood up, she would have banged her head on the ceiling and blocked out most of the light in the room.

Some of the artists' models didn't look too normal, either. Jane Morris, the wife of William Morris, was a devoted friend and model for

Rossetti after his wife, Elizabeth Siddal, committed suicide. She was also much flattered by his portrayal of her. In real life (as can be seen from contemporary photographs), she was heavy-featured, her hair growing down low on her forehead, her features causing foreigners to laugh at her when she was abroad. But there is something else about her that invites comment; her peculiar neck, to some learned eyes, shows definite signs of a goiter.

Highly strung as they were, some artists made themselves ill through love, or bad temper. Jean-François de Troy was so distraught at being parted from his mistress and sent back to France that he slumped into silence and promptly died of grief. Pietro Torrigiano (the gentleman who reconstructed Michelangelo's profile with a mallet) was always an argumentative man, and whereas most people would have been terrified to fall into the hands of the Inquisition, Torrigiano was bloody *outraged* and starved himself to death as a protest!

Luckily, artists are human, and they suffer from the same illnesses and humiliating symptoms as the rest of humanity. Gustave Courbet, for instance, underwent an operation for his hemorrhoids, and when it wasn't a total success, he cut down the trees outside his privy so that he could sit there for hours and look out, saying, 'I'll never be one of those base persons to resign themselves to staring a whole hour in a shed!'

The sixteenth-century Italian painter Pontormo, also suffered from illness, real and imaginary. A troubled, nervous artist, he wrote a diary that tells us of his loneliness, his absorption with work — and the day-by-day function of his bowels. Others complained of their health — Bernini endured repeated migraines; Gustave Doré suffered from indigestion; Michelangelo developed a goiter while working on the Sistine Chapel, and Gainsborough suffered from cancer.

The list is endless: Reynolds was deaf; Millais suffered with his nerves; George Frederick Watts was a hypochondriac who was always fretting about his health and how the temperature affected it; Renoir's hands were so crippled with arthritis that his brushes had to be strapped to his fingers so that he could paint; and Hendrick Avercamp was so sullen that he became known as 'The Dumb Man.'

Others were careless with their health: Fra Bartolommeo always worked under a window where the sunlight poured in and fell straight onto his back. After a number of years, this finally paralyzed him down one side and so, being incapacitated, he turned to eating for consolation. During his convalescence, he became more and more bored and kept consuming more and more fruit — which did nothing for his constitution. In the end, a vast meal of figs, combined with his existing malady, sent him off to his Maker with indecent haste.

Other artists were not very prepossessing in appearance: Munnings had one eye; Turner was short, with a hooked nose; Diaz had a wooden leg; Toulouse-Lautrec was no taller than a dwarf; Guernico had crossed eyes; Michelangelo had a broken nose (as well as a problem with his personal hygiene); Vincent Van Gogh had one ear, and Solario was a hunchback.

But the last word on illness must go to Michelangelo. Working under appalling conditions in the Sistine Chapel, he created one of the world's masterpieces. However, it cost him dearly in terms of health, as he described in his own words:

While doing this work I've grown a goiter like the cats get from the water in Lombardy . . . and my belly has been forced to stick to my chin . . . from the air above me, my paintbrush drips down onto my face, turning me into a rich pavement . . . My loins dig into my belly and to counterbalance this I thrust out my arse like a crupper . . . I feel unwell in this place.

7

The Occult

In past centuries, the occult was generally more accepted than it is today. The Indians had the palms and feet of their children read at birth, and the English, Italian, Greek, and French had their horoscopes cast to predict what the future held. By these means, it was believed, misfortune could be avoided and good fortune assured. But the occult also encompassed the black arts, Satanism and alchemy, and many artists painted scenes of the occult, some even indulging in such practices in their own lives.

Alchemy, the turning of base metal into gold, has intrigued painters for centuries. There are many famous paintings, such as *The Alchemist* by Cornelis Bega, that illustrate the practice. Indeed, some artists actually attempted alchemy in their own lives, possibly in the belief that magic would provide them with more money than art.

Goya, of course, was one of the chief painters of the occult, his deafness helping him turn to inward and create monsters, and he himself wrote on the back of one of the plates of *Los Caprichos* that 'the sleep of reason produces monsters.'

As he grew older, his interest extended to a form of interior decor that had nothing in common with Laura Ashley. Wall after wall in his house, he decorated with the so-called black paintings, which included scenes of black magic, tombs, and visions of levitating witches.

Even his religious paintings have a flavor of the occult, and his *Procession of Flagellants*, with its depiction of the bloody backs of the flagellants, naked from the waist up, their heads covered in cloth masks, is very disturbing — as are the clerics who surround them in their black robes and black pointed hats.

As a religious theme this seems threatening, although it is not as overtly unpleasant as *The Witches' Sabbath*. Bearing in mind that these pictures were based on *real happenings, The Witches' Sabbath* is repulsive, with a smiling goat (the form the Devil took when he showed himself) sitting in the middle of the circle of admirers. Further scrutiny reveals more unpleasant details, again based on reality — the mother holding out her struggling baby as an offering to the devil; the old crone handling a skeletal child, its sticklike arms at odds with the corpulent worshipers who surround it; and, worst of all, one child, greeny-gray, lying dead and unnoticed between two women, one of whom holds a stick from which hang three dead infants. Children were actually sacrificed to the Devil in some rites.

Satanism was rife in Spain and employed by people of all classes — by the poor to give them some power, by the rich to obliterate their rivals. One of Goya's other notorious occult paintings is *Saturn*, which is one of the blackest images in art. In it, Goya depicts Saturn literally eating one of his children (a sobering thought, as the painter hung it in his dining room), the specter's livid red tongue licking and ripping off the top of his victim's torso, his hands digging into the flesh as he grips his prey. In a country well used to the Inquisition, similar horrors were not unknown.

Italy was a superstitious country, too, especially in the late sixteenth century, and it was a common occurrence for someone to refer to a person as being 'bedeviled.' Pordenone was an artist who worked at the same time as Titian, but that was the only thing they had in common. Where Titian was sophisticated and easygoing, Pordenone was quarrelsome and solitary.

His work rate was formidable. On one occasion, he was commissioned by a patron to paint a Madonna, and worked so fast that he had it finished by the time the buyer returned from mass. Another time, he completed a fresco so quickly that the townspeople thought he had been helped by the Devil.

Perhaps he *was* in league with Satan. He certainly seemed overmotivated and unable to rest, moving constantly from one city to another, and marrying three times, his wives apparently boring him as quickly as everything else did. Pordenone's talent for fighting was legendary as well, and he took offense as easily as most people take breath.

Unfortunately, as he grew older, Pordenone's activities became more serious and his reputation for being 'bedeviled' grew. He fought his own brother in a duel over their father's will, and was then responsible for his friend's death when they were involved in a fight. The last record of this spooky man relates how he lost a commission to Titian and, infuriated, went around telling everyone that Titian had sworn to kill him. Curiously enough, Titian never set eyes on him again, and neither did anyone else. From that day onward, Pordenone disappeared without trace.

Occultism was still rife in Italy in the eighteenth century, and was illustrated by artists such as Tiepolo, whose occult pictures such as *Two Magicians and a Boy* were always popular. This drawing shows us a youth having his horoscope cast. Next to where he stands, a group of skulls and snakes lie in untidy piles, and an owl (to some a symbol of evil) watches from a tree. This was a period in history when patrons included the occult as a part of their lives, and they frequently had their fortunes read and horoscopes cast, or commissioned occult paintings.

As the centuries passed, the occult did lose some of its stranglehold, but it still continued to intrigue a group of painters who developed into the Symbolists. The nineteenth-century Belgian painter Félicien Rops tried to make a career out of being sensational, and in his series *Les Sataniques*, he manages to go the whole nine yards and mix Satanism with pornography. In one painting, *The Monsters*, a pack of phallic symbols lurches out of a murky pond in a ludicrous attempt at the sinister.

Salvator Rosa was also fascinated by occultism and witchcraft, as his painting *Witches at Their Incantations* shows. This picture, in the National Gallery, London, shows us what *really* happened at a Satanist Sabbath. Already the participants have summoned up a ghoulish monster on the right of the painting, and a naked, bloated witch in the center holds a wax effigy that has been mutilated with pins. The theory behind this was that where the pin was stuck into the victim, an injury would occur. Behind this witch is a man holding out a heart pierced with a sword, and a burned rabbit smolders on a paper beside them.

In the days when this picture was painted, it was believed that witches at a Sabbath could bring the dead back to life, and on the far left we see one revived corpse covered by a sheet, while another looms out of its coffin, a witch guiding its skeletal hand to write on the paper in front of him. To cap it all, there is a hanged man swinging from a tree in the middle of the painting, his face distorted and blue, and his neck broken. As with a great many occult practices, the practitioners believed that the hair and nails of the dead could be used in black-magic rites. Look closely at the shadowed space under the hanged man and you can just make out a witch cutting the dead man's toenails.

Occultism with a healthy dash of sex has never gone amiss, and sometimes the most shocking depictions are not the modern ones. Consider *The Devil Showing Woman to the People* by Otto Greiner. This drawing was done in 1897 and still has the power to shock the onlooker. Similarly, the creepy *Rape* by Max Klinger has more to do with bedevilment than seduction. It is a curious piece, a woman's arms stretching out through the broken glass of her window to what appears to be a pterodactyl flying off with one evening glove. It would be amusing, but for the relentlessly bleak atmosphere.

Occultism takes many forms — the obvious, such as Goya's witches, and the less obvious, such as G. F. Watts's *Minotaur*, a weird picture that shows the solitary beast looking out with rapt attention over a desolate landscape. The minotaur has long persisted in art, as a creature combining sexual and occult energy. The Devil naturally comes in many disguises, one of them being the Sphinx, a figure of magical power who has fascinated artists from Ingres to Franz von Stuck. The latter depicted his hero caught by *The Kiss of the Sphinx*, who is leaning over him and appears to be sucking his life's breath away. There is a potent feeling of destruction in this, as there is in Burne-Jones's painting *The Beguiling of Merlin*, in which the magician is looking decidedly uneasy, having received a taste of his own medicine.

The Swiss artist Fuseli was obviously obsessed by the occult, and by dreams. His drawings were as eccentric as he was, his female types repeated over and over again, their hair adorned in odd phallic shapes, their figures as idealized as an airbrush drawing in a magazine. It is only when he lets his imagination run riot that Fuseli produces incredible paintings such as *Macbeth and the Witches*, in which a trio of hags, all in profile, point into the distance, somewhere off frame.

Fuseli also loved Shakespeare, his own mind offering up dramatic and eerie images that he had no trouble putting onto canvas. His *Lady Macbeth Seizes the Daggers* is created almost entirely in black and white, Lady Macbeth snatching the weapons from her husband with the expression of someone who has just found her child carving its initials on the pianoforte. Macbeth cringes back — as well as he might — and the only bit of color in the whole picture is the bloodred of his stomach and chest, which appear to have been skinned, the muscle wall exposed to the viewer.

Fuseli could never resist an opportunity to shock. When he illustrated Shakespeare, it was with a very original eye, and even his *Botton and Titania* is startingly different from the norm. Here we have the ass-headed Bottom sitting with the fairy queen, while around this ill-matched couple hovers a selection of creatures that would have done credit to Hieronymus Bosch. On the right of the painting is a woman walking an old elf on a lead and in front of him is a cowled, dwarflike figure holding a nude goblin. And then, if you peer into the painting, you can find a fairy child with an insect's tongue and huge winglike ears.

Curious as this painting is, Fuseli's most famous picture must still be the peculiar *The Nightmare*. This depicts a woman dreaming, her thoughts producing an incubus, a creature that descends on sleeping people. This malevolent form is stout and hairy, and sits, bearing down on her chest, while a ghost horse peers between the bed curtains. With a lesser artist, it could have looked like a poster for a circus, but Fuseli pulls the image off with real skill. Incidentally, Sigmund Freud had a copy of this painting hanging in his study.

Why has no one depicted the succubus, the female demon who has sexual intercourse with sleeping men? Perhaps this is too much of a nightmare for male artists and explains why the nearest we get to it is the all-devouring mermaid in Böcklin's supernatural *Calm Sea*, who watches her exhausted and sexually beguiled mate drift away from her under a deep and threatening sea.

Unfortunately, for some the occult led to madness — as Richard Dadd, a nineteenth-century English painter, found to his cost. Fascinated by magic, he painted many strange depictions of fairies and elves, such as *The Fairy Feller's Master-Stroke*, pictures that are peopled with diminutive ugly dwarfs and curious women. Unfortunately, dwelling on such things did Dadd no good, and, after killing his father, he was committed as a lunatic for the rest of his life.

The subject of clairvoyance and fortune-telling has always been popular, and has been depicted throughout the centuries — the eternal need to know about the future as irresistible for the artists as for the rest of humanity. Even Caravaggio took time off from his usual religious epics to paint *The Fortune Teller* — partly because it was a popular subject and easy to sell, and partly because he was Italian, and the Italians had two hobbies at that time: predicting and poisoning.

Charles Ricketts had no interest in palmistry; his occult curiosity was altogether more weird. A famous example that shows us the devastating power of the other world is his picture *The Death of Don Juan*. This painting shows the hero lurching back as the ghost of the Commander tells him his chips are up. Don Juan looks sick, not without reason, but the picture was a giant success, the character's refusal to repent his lusty deeds in the face of death appealing to the maverick taste of the time.

An altogether stranger painting of this era is *The Turkey*, by the German painter Alfred Kubin. Although its appeal relies heavily on the occult, the image of a woman perched on a lump of rock with a turkey at her feet resembles little more than a host's nightmare at having forgotten to order the Christmas lunch.

The nineteenth-century art world was soon caught up with the occult, the taste of the day favoring the heady ménage à trois of sex, religion, and mysticism. Henry Singleton turned to Shakespeare for his inspiration, and his painting *Ariel on a Bat's Back* is memorable, to put it mildly. Here we have a character, Ariel, being transported on the back of a creature only slightly smaller than a DC-10.

William Blake, as we already have seen, was either highly imaginative or completely mad.

173

Either way, he was smart enough to communicate with the dead and carry on long conversations with them without the benefit of AT&T. His old friend, the flea, falls into this category of mystical dialogue, and his contemporary Varley described the scene when Blake was drawing the insect: 'Blake was interrupted by the flea opening its mouth, which he then drew separately, finishing the main head when the flea obligingly closed its mouth again.'

Ghosts In Paintings

When an artist corrects something he has already painted, he paints over it. After a while, this underpainting sometimes shows through, giving a 'ghosting' effect. This is called pentimento — from the Italian 'to repent,' as the artist has 'repented' his first thought.

VAN DYCK: **William Fielding, First Earl of Denbigh (National Gallery, London)**
The young black boy servant has two sets of lips.

Queen Henrietta Maria (Her Majesty the Queen)
A ghost hand holds a scarf on the right of the painting.

Thomas Wentworth, First Earl of Strafford (Trustees of the Rt. Hon. Olive, Countess Fitzwilliam's Chattels settlement) Two right legs.

GABRIEL METSU: **Woman Peeling Apples** (Louvre, Paris) The rabbit has two heads.

VELÁZQUEZ: **Portrait of a Lady with a Fan** (Wallace Collection, London)
The woman's head and shoulders have been moved over to the right and blurred like a photographic image.

Calabazas (Prado, Madrid)

This painting is full of ghosts. The bottle on the right has two tops, and the cape of Calabazas can be seen miraculously through the bottle on the left.

Philip IV as a Hunter (Prado, Madrid)
There are two right legs, and a phantom hat. Obviously Velázquez put the hat on Philip's head after it had been originally painted in his left hand.

Philip IV, Equestrian (Prado, Madrid)
The horse has two left-hind legs, two right-hind hooves, and Philip has a ghost scarf on his left shoulder.

Philip IV (Prado, Madrid)
An impressive portrait, with its phantom cloak that billows out — making Philip look as though he weighed at least 280 pounds.

Philip IV (National Gallery, London)
The left table leg is coming through the cloak of Philip IV.

PIETER DE HOOCH: **Woman Drinking with Two Men and a Maidservant** (National Gallery, London)
The lower half of the woman in front of the fireplace is transparent. The black and white floor is ghosting through her skirt, and the drinker on the left is beginning to turn into the invisible man, too, as his cloak is transparent.

CASPAR NETSCHER: **Chaff Cutter with a**

Woman Spinning and a Young Boy (John G. Johnson Collection, Philadelphia Museum of Art)
Times must certainly have been hard for this family. The young boy, according to the ghost figure that surrounds him, has shrunk with all the hard work and has lost several inches and a few pounds.

VERONESE: **The Family of Darius Before Alexander** (National Gallery, London)
There are two ghost horses in the left-hand background.

MILLAIS: **Lorenzo and Isabella** (Walker Art Gallery, Liverpool)
On the left-hand side are a pair of crossed feet in red tights with a pair of ghost feet under them. This is particularly interesting, as the ghost feet touch the floor and the others don't.

JOHN WRIGHT: **Sir Brooke Boothby** (Tate Gallery, London) This gentleman is reclining by a brook. Unfortunately, a large plant is ghosting through his trousers.

8

Artists' Wives, Families, and Lovers

As you would expect, artists attract some people and repulse others. Perhaps it's the heady combination of talent and bloody-mindedness, or simply a glamour that pulls people to them, but either way, many an artist's family has had a rough ride, and many a love affair has burned out in the time it took for a canvas to dry.

Modigliani loved women and used them, as did Titian, but other painters had the misfortune to fall in love, and some actually wanted to lead ordinary lives. For the sake of posterity, however, they had the good fortune to marry hopelessly unsuitable mates. Andrea del Sarto was the perfect example of a man with huge talent being driven into the ground by a woman.

Signora del Sarto was stupid and beautiful, a deadly combination at the best of times. She was also jealous of her husband and did not like the idea that he should paint anyone else. So from the day of their marriage onward, scores of identical Virgin Marys swamped Italy, like latter-day Warhol Marilyns. In return for all this free publicity, Signora del Sarto refused admittance to her husband's friends, was consistently unpleasant, and, in a bad error of judgment, would not allow Andrea to return to Francis I in France to explain how they had spent the money he foolishly had advanced them.

Not known for his sense of humor, Francis threatened torture from a distance while Andrea hid in Italy, driven to exasperation by the woman with whom he was infatuated. In the end, the plague caught up with him and, although his condition was beyond help, his wife was beyond reason. Not willing to nurse her husband, she left Andrea del Sarto to die alone — no doubt heartily relieved to be left in peace at last.

Many wives hindered their husband's careers. Mrs. Hoppner, for example, was a woman with little patience and, although her husband was in competition with Reynolds, she could not control her temper. Dear, deaf old Reynolds loved children and played with them when they came for sittings, no doubt making sure that the family would note his kindliness and send the next little offspring to be painted. But Mrs. Hoppner did *not* like children, and when they were sent to her husband, their likenesses weren't the only thing to be struck. At first, they were encouraged to sit down and be quiet, but, if persuasion failed, Mrs. Hoppner then took up a whip to press the point home. Needless to say, Mr. Hoppner painted few children — and even less when his wife was about.

If Reynolds was charming with his patrons' children, he was a little less than kind with his own relations. His sister Frances acted as his unpaid housekeeper for years and although her own works of art were exhibited and praised, her brother resented the copies she made of his pictures. In a rush of characteristic boorishness, he snapped, 'They make other people laugh, and me cry.'

One can only presume that he watched his food for a while after making that remark.

Another of his sisters, Elizabeth, had problems that embarrassed Reynolds — and Reynolds hated to be embarrassed. Elizabeth's husband was the Mayor of Torrington, but, possibly due to the pressure of high office, he upped and left his wife and children to live with another woman. While thus engaged, he lost Elizabeth's money, then his own, then some of Reynolds's (a matter that Elizabeth was never allowed to forget). But she had guts, and succeeded in raising her children by her own efforts; when her husband returned home seriously ill, Elizabeth nursed him until he died. (Reynolds never got his money back.)

Some of the most unlikely men attract undying devotion, even without asking for it. The fifteenth-century Flemish artist Robert Campin was unstable, hysterical, and unrealiable long before it became a fashion. After succeeding as a painter, he was fined for an unspecified crime, forced to go on a pilgrimage, and forbidden to hold any high civic office. For four years, he lay low, and then his erratic temperament got the better of him again. This time, he was banished for leading a debauched life, and was saved from further disgrace by the intervention of an anonymous wealthy countess, who interceded on the painter's behalf, and because she loved him, managed to have his sentence reduced to a fine.

No one knew who the countess was or what

became of her although everyone knew exactly what happened to the wife of Alonso Cano. As a painter, Cano was successful, but he was a fool with money and in 1636 he was thrown into prison for debt. Incredibly enough, he still managed to infiltrate the court (as in kings, not judges) the following year and was doing very nicely indeed until his wife was found stabbed. As the prime suspect, Cano was arrested but finally acquitted, even though no one else was charged with her murder.

Love can bring out the worst in people, and Rembrandt, for all his greatness, was not above a mean trick. After his wife's death, he hired a housekeeper who would also act as a nurse for his son, Titus. Her name was Geertge Dircx, and apparently she soon moved from the kitchen to the bedroom and became the artist's mistress. Unfortunately, she also became something of a nuisance to Rembrandt, and, after Hendrickje Stoffels arrived, Rembrandt avoided his promise of marriage to Geertge, and had her committed to a 'house of correction' instead. After this, there was no record of her, although Hendrickje was obviously made of sterner stuff. Having removed her rival, she soon occupied the position the unfortunate Geertje so recently had vacated, and Hendrickje stayed until she died.

The Pre-Raphaelite Brotherhood also had trouble with their affairs of the heart. Holman Hunt was besotted with John Millais, and even gave him a ring when they were separated, but after Millais married, he looked around for some female companionship instead and had an affair with his model, Annie Miller. Unfortunately, he had chosen a vicious woman, whom Rossetti described as 'destructive,' and who showed her real nature after their affair was over.

In true tabloid style, she threatened to expose Holman Hunt's love letters and have them published in the newspapers, a move that would have ruined his career. Luckily, he avoided such an outcome by a bit of clever footwork. But he never had much luck with his women and he never learned any discretion. After his first wife died in childbirth, he married her sister, causing a national scandal.

Rossetti didn't fare much better. In his case, he fell in love with the beautiful Elizabeth Siddal, and used her as a model and muse. It should have stopped there, but they married and he began to take her for granted, having affairs and generally behaving badly. Their home was cold and depressing, and he neglected her, even becoming entangled with the man-eating Annie Miller. In the end, Elizabeth became a drug addict, and died from the effects of her addiction.

In a state of grief and guilt, Rossetti drew back from the world and became a recluse. He moved to Cheyne Walk to escape her memory and began to collect animals, and as he withdrew from humans, he relied on four-legged companions. At one time, he had kangaroos, lizards, wombats, and a bull for company, his reclusive existence and menagerie no doubt exciting a fair amount of gossip from the neighbors.

The only person he continued to love was Jane

Morris, with whom he carried on an extensive correspondence. The affair was always platonic, but it provided Rossetti with a lifeline as he slipped further and further into decay, drink, and drugs — chloral (at one point, he was taking 180 grams a day), laudanum, and injections of morphia. He finally died from his addictions, taking the same route his wife had taken all those years before.

Jane Morris was obviously exceptional, and a genuine muse, both for Rossetti and her husband, William Morris, who wrote on his canvas as he painted her: 'I cannot paint you but I love you.'

Working-class and simple, she was the daughter of an ostler, but she somehow managed to inspire these artists by her presence, and, when her marriage to Morris went flat, she was kind and compassionate to the ailing Rossetti until he died.

Rossetti was a dashing man — at least in his youth — whereas Burne-Jones looks like a sad little fellow. But then, appearances can be deceiving; certainly the volatile and handsome Mary Zambaco found something deeply attractive in the artist, and pursued him with all the passion of her Greek blood. The talk of London, their ten-year affair was conducted openly and shamelessly, even though both of them were married.

When Burne-Jones finally decided to give Mary up for his wife and children, she responded quite reasonably by throwing herself into the Thames. Unfortunately, this kind of behavior can be guaranteed to excite notice; soon the police arrived, and there was a tremendous scandal, followed by Mary Zambaco's total nervous collapse.

A few words written to her from him many years later tell the story:

> Dear ill-used friend,
> You must believe . . . I never forget you . . . come back some day and write and say you forgive.

Mary Zambaco read it and did what any sensible woman would do — she sighed, remembered, and then set her sights on another artist: Rodin.

Leonardo had little interest in women: His mind moved more to men, or boys, to be precise. In Florence he was denounced for sodomy, even though practicing homosexuality was punishable by being burned at the stake if he repented. If he didn't, he was bound for hell, according to the religious authorities. Brilliant at most things, Leonardo was no judge of character, a fact made patently obvious when he employed the fabulously handsome Salai as his general drudge. He then compounded the felony by falling in love with this feckless layabout, who, realizing that he had a sucker at his beck and call, stole from Leonardo, lied to him, and threw every kindness back into his face. The effect his shortcomings had on his beauty is well known, as Leonardo's sketches show the decline from pretty boy to puffy, sweet-eating hedonist. His antics must have become intolerable, though, as even the smitten painter was forced to write of him: 'thief, obstinate, glutton.'

Yet though his patience was stretched to the limit with this appalling, untalented youth, Leonardo kept him constantly beside him and, forgiving to the end, remembered him in his will.

★ ★ ★

It is generally dangerous to be obsessed by anything, yet many artists became obsessed by their models, and their art became stamped with the personality and face of one person. Such a painter was Fernand Khnopff, a Belgian, who was fastidious about detail, in his life, his clothes, his food, and his art. His whole life was studied perfection, and yet his imagination was weird and unreal. In his symbolistic pictures, he painted his sister repeatedly in peculiar poses. Once her head was stuck onto the torso of a leopard, another time her noggin emerges out of the body of what appears to be a gigantic pigeon. Indeed, after a while, the brother and sister become almost indistinguishable from each other.

The prim Victorian painter, G. F. Watts, would not have approved of such things. He was too Victorian for that. Yet even he managed to shock everyone when he announced that he was finally going to marry — especially as his bride happened to be an actress of only 16 years of age. After several disappointments in love, Watts was lonely and desperately in need of a wife. Ellen Terry, however, was little more to him than a charming ornament and the marriage was doomed from the start.

In a letter to Bernard Shaw, she wrote, ' . . . Mr. Watts kissed me in the studio one day and then I was engaged to him and all the rest of it . . . and then he kissed me — differently — not much differently but a little . . . but when I was alone with Mother . . . I told her I must be married *now* because I was going to have a baby!!! and she believed me . . . '

One can just imagine the pure unadulterated joy her mother must have felt on hearing the splendid news. Anyway, they did marry, and after such a start everything else must have been a ghastly disappointment, because soon it was obvious to everyone that the marriage was a disaster. Suggestions flew about that G. F. Watts was impotent, but it was never proved, and when the marriage finally ended, Ellen Terry went on to become a very respected actress, mixing with the likes of Irving, while Watts went back to mixing colors.

Heartache was not restricted to English artists. Mieris the Elder had experienced his own problems in seventeenth-century Holland. Born into a family of *twenty-three* children, he trained as an artist and specialized in genre painting, which isn't surprising, considering his background. What *was* surprising was that, after a hasty retreat from his brothers and sisters, Mieris decided to get married — thereby ensuring the lack of privacy he had so far enjoyed.

They found a house and settled down happily. His wife was content and she liked the town of

Leiden. She liked Leiden so much, in fact, that when the Archduke Leopold William did her husband the great honor of inviting him to Vienna, she refused to go with him, even though she knew he would not go alone. 'Please,' Mieris begged. 'Not likely,' she replied.

And so another brilliant career went down the tubes, thanks to the painter's family.

Goya's emotional life was hazardous, too. Because of an indiscreet love affair, the Inquistion became interested in him, and he left Madrid to go and live in the 'deaf man's house' with his mistress, Leocadia, who was related by marriage to Goya's son. After a while, she bore Goya a daughter and everything was just fine, except for the Inquisition, which did not like anyone having a good time — especially with their own relative, no matter how distant.

Goya's libido flagged under the threat of torture and, after considerable difficulties, he managed to get his mistress and daughter to Bordeaux, where they could live safely. A reliable and faithful man, he then spent a number of years leaping between the two countries like a ping-pong ball, finally dying in exile, aged eighty-two.

You would think that after looking after his family so well, they would reciprocate in some way. His beloved grandson, Mariano, was bequeathed the 'deaf man's house' and most of Goya's paintings to keep for posterity. Regrettably, posterity held little attraction for the wayward Mariano, and he sold all the paintings with indecent haste, buying himself a title with the proceeds.

Worse things befell some artists, who escaped from appalling marriages only to fall into other hopeless situations. Pierre-Paul Prud'hon, whose career glittered alongside David's, was dogged by the ghastly wife he had married when he was nineteen. Naturally, he sought solace with someone who understood him better than she did, and, with a stupendous stroke of originality, he fell for one of his pupils, Constance Mayer, who was lovely but incapable of living up to her Christian name. After a turbulent eighteen-year liaison, she finally committed suicide in Prud'hon's studio — the trauma of her death wiping him out as efficiently as a speeding fiveton truck.

Another well-known fact is that artists seldom work happily together. The jealousy and rivalry usually forbids close friendship, and it is even more rare for a husband and wife to work together. Richard Conway was a well-known dandy, a friend of the future George IV, and a very skilful miniature painter. His wife, Maria Hadfield, was no less remarkable, and although she was not as gifted, they managed to live and work together happily. They also prospered and became successful. Naturally, this success meant money, and money meant a kind of lifestyle usually adopted by talk-show hosts and rock stars.

Their notorious goings-on attracted frenzied gossip, their house and visitors engaging everyone's curiosity for years. But the scandal died with the death of Richard Conway and the departure of his lusty wife to Italy. There, neither she nor her late husband were well known, and every trace of her previous lifestyle was well hidden

— which probably accounts for the fact that she managed to secure a job as a headmistress, running a girls' school until her death.

But although Maria Hadfield survived her marriage, Ribera is the perfect example of an artist brought down and ruined by his family. At first, everything went well for him. His work was fashionable and in demand in Naples, and his life was blessed with the affection of the people, his nickname 'Il Spagnoletto,' referring to the fact that he was a bit on the short side and rather cute.

He did have a gloomy side, however, and his depictions of torture leave little to the imagination. His use of bitumen (a medium that darkens on the canvas dramatically) means that his somber and often brutal paintings have taken on an even more gloomy quality, the various brutalities taking place in what appears to be a cellar lit by a forty-watt bulb.

Anyway, be that as it may, Ribera's life went from success to success — until the bastard son of Philip IV set eyes on his daughter. Don Juan, as he was called (this is *not* a joke), fell heavily in love and managed to seduce the girl — triumph for Don Juan; tragedy for Ribera.

Marriage was out of the question, and as the seducer had bragged and advertised his conquest with the kind of subtlety usually reserved for the tabloids, Ribera's daughter was ruined, as was her father. The trauma made him ill and slowed down his work, so that in his last years, Ribera's reputation floundered as surely as his daughter's had done. He died heartbroken, and she remained unmarried.

It is now apparent that these artists did not choose their women, or their relations, well. Sometimes this was due to bad luck, at other times due to bad judgment, but the one thing that seems obvious is that most couples were mismatched. Or, to put it another way, God makes them, and the Devil pairs them.

The famous portrait painter Anthony van Dyck demonstrates this perfectly. By nature fragile and easily exhausted, he still managed to fall in love with Margaret Lemon, and he took her as his mistress. She *was* beautiful, which helped, but she was also possessive, had a tongue as sour as her name, and was possessed of a hysterical nature that must have been a considerable drain on her lover's energies.

Her jealousy was notorious throughout London. Hollar described her as 'a dangerous woman,' and there were rumors that she had been a prostitute before meeting van Dyck. In fact, things got so bad between the two lovers that, after one particularly violent argument, Margaret Lemon bit through van Dyck's thumb in an attempt to prevent him from painting any other women. It was a nasty, childish act and reckless — after all, she was risking her wealthy lifestyle with one chomp of her molars.

But in the end, the exhausting Margaret proved too much for van Dyck and, after a towering argument, he deserted her in order to marry the quiet Mary Ruthven, securing a peaceful life and the safety of his remaining fingers.

Artists And Their Pets

It might give an interesting insight into some of the painters to know that they loved their animals. And what a variety of animals!

Hogarth:
A dog, Vulcan, and a pug dog, Trump.

Gainsborough:
Dogs.

Sodoma:
A talking raven, an ape, hens,
and doves.

Rossetti:
Wombat, bull, kangaroo, lizard,
and a racoon.

Reynolds:
Parrot.

Leonardo:
Bought birds at the market to set them free.

Rosso:
A Barbary ape and a horse.

Van Gogh:
A mouse.

Otto Marseus Van Schriek:
Insects and snakes.

Rembrandt:
A small monkey.

9

The Sitters

It is greatly to our advantage that when we read about the great men and women of history, we also can scrutinize their portraits, relying on a variety of artists to breathe life into them. At a time when photography or television news did not exist, people relied on artists to depict the VIPs. Richard III had six portraits painted in order that these pictures might travel throughout the kingdom to show the provincial peasants what they were missing.

Portrait painting has always been lucrative and informative; Gainsborough painted many a whore as a goddess and many a coward as a gallant soldier. Early on in his career, the portrait painter who wishes to succeed should discover how to flatter, unless, like Hogarth or Daumier, he wishes to earn his living by satire. This is not a course of action to be recommended, unless the artist wishes to spend some time languishing under various majesties' displeasure — both Hogarth and Daumier spent time in jail, Daumier serving six months for his notorious caricature 'Gargantua swallowing bags of gold extorted from the people,' which depicted King Louis Philippe.

It was a much safer bet to paint the great and good as the great and good wished to be portrayed. Godfrey Kneller was a superb example of an artist who flattered everyone, giving every sitter's portrait the psychological insight of a pickled walnut. Titian played the same game, but occasionally painted a wonderfully honest portrait, such as the one of Aretino.

This remarkable man loved intrigue, sex, and depravity. A member of the court, he was unpleasant, vicious, and vitriolic about everyone, so much so that one wit remarked, 'He never spoke ill of God — but that was only because he had never met Him.'

Aretino's shady career began early. At thirteen, he turned his hand to petty theft and, after mugging his mother, he left for Rome. On arrival, he looked for protectors and was taken on by the Pope; in this powerful position Aretino turned his mind to blackmail. For years, he dug up the dirt on everyone, demanding presents in return for his silence, and was so feared that monarchs such as Henry VIII and the Holy Roman Emperor Charles V spent vast sums of money to keep his vitriolic pen pointing in someone else's direction.

The letters he wrote to his victims after they had paid up make fascinating reading: 'For the fine and excellent turkey which the affable kindness of your true courtesy sent me from Padua, I give you as many thanks as it had feathers.'

As with many villains, this charmless man continued to prosper and was rewarded handsomely, Francis I presenting him with a gold chain whose links were fashioned in the shape of poisonous tongues. But Aretino made too many enemies and, at the time Titian was painting his portrait, someone attacked him. He was stabbed and lost most of the use of his right hand, so for the rest of his life he had to write holding his pen between his thumb and his last two fingers. One doubts that this would have helped his temper any.

His end was in keeping with his life, and in a memorable stroke of irony, Aretino choked to death laughing too much at a joke — which for once turned out to be at his expense.

Another of Titian's troublesome sitters was Ippolito de' Medici, who had been made a cardinal at seventeen by his uncle, Pope Clement VII. Apparently this was done to try to prevent Ippolito from killing his cousin, Alessandro, and to instill some sense in him. But Ippolito was as ungovernable as ever, and, when the Turks invaded Hungary, he set off to beat them. Unfortunately, although he succeeded in saving the Hungarians, Ippolito also looted them, and indulged in a fair amount of raping and plundering while he was about it.

In despair, Emperor Charles V had him put in irons, and this apparently taught Ippolito a lesson. After he was released, he calmed down and then set about making a home for himself, creating a palace that made Charles's court look like a housing estate. The Pope, not unreasonably, asked him to drop some of this three hundred lackeys. But an offended Ippolito declined, saying, 'I do not need them — they need me.'

His end was as lurid as his life. Caught in a plan to blow the unfortunate Alessandro into a thousand assorted bits, Ippolito fled, but finally was taken by the oldest enemy of them all — poison.

Ippolito would probably have got on well with William, Lord Byron, as they had a lot in common. This man was an English collector whose passion for paintings decreased as his love of the booze increased, his drinking bringing tragedy when he killed a relation in a drunken duel. Calling on his rights, he was tried in the House of Lords, and acquitted. From then on his only occupation was as a professional recluse, although he once did rouse himself sufficiently to ruin his own son's life.

The boy married against his father's wishes, and his father resented it so much that he sold off all the family treasures, let the gardens become overgrown, and left the house to rot under him until it become worthless. The only pity is that it never fell in and buried him alive, but he died of natural causes, his epitaph describing him accurately and damningly as 'Devil Byron.'

But the right kind of notoriety can guarantee a portrait's success, and can also be good for business — the artist's and the sitter's. Even the priggish G. F. Watts forced himself to paint the royal mistress, Lillie Langtry, and he did not appear to suffer from the flock of influential clients who followed, and many a Victorian artist painted the voluptuous charms of Egyptian dancing girls, apparently oblivious to the fact that these dancers earned their livings horizontally as well as vertically. Caught up in the magic of the East, they did not comprehend the reality of the life they were painting; one of the almah's traditional dances, the 'bee,' was the origin of the striptease as we know it today.

Groups of painters such as the Orientalists were visually seduced by the countries they visited, painting innumerable harem women, scenes in Turkish baths, and the garishly clothed mercenaries. As sitters, each of these people provided an exotic, powerful image that still fascinates; indeed the whirling dervishes painted by Gérôme ate glowing embers, live serpents, and glass — before breakfast.

Likewise, it is hard to believe that George Selwyn, who was painted by Reynolds, was capable of 'sentimental sodomy' with various members of the upper crust. His languid expression might indicate his tendency to nod off in the House of Commons, but his addiction to gambling is not obvious in the limp face. Impervious to women as Mr. Selwyn undoubtedly was, he became extremely famous in time for another, less physical, passion — a love of public executions.

Not that *all* sitters were tramps or reprobates; the occasional hero does emerge. Such was Captain the Hon. John Hamilton, painted by Reynolds. This gentleman was lieutenant of the *Louisa*, a ship that was inconveniently wrecked in a howling gale. As the crew was being rescued, Hamilton declined to leave, insisting that all men go first and that he would be the last to be taken off. Unfortunately, his seafaring luck ran out in a very embarrassing way. In Portsmouth Harbour on a blissfully still summer day, Captain Hamilton was making the short ran from his ship to the shore — and sank. His boat overturned and he drowned without leaving so much as a ripple to mark his end.

Other stalwart types had their portraits done. Richard Burton (the famous explorer, not the Welsh actor) was a man who disliked his native country. In his insatiable need for travel and experience, he descended upon Cairo. Now this was 1854, long before package tours and the 'just hold this and I'll get a shot of you by the pyramid' mentality. This was *old* Cairo, where the food killed you if the natives didn't.

Into this merry scenario came Richard Burton, duly disguised in full Arab dress and sporting a 'you can speak Egyptian in three days' vocabulary. Meanwhile the painter Thomas Seddon had just arrived with Holman Hunt, and all three of them met up. Interestingly, although Burton was not a vain man, he *was* proud of the fact that he had infiltrated Mecca by posing as a doctor from India and he wanted some kind of commemoration for the folks back home.

The resulting portrait is wonderful, and no doubt brought even more fame to our hero. Unfortunately, the artist did not fare so well from *his* sojourn in Arabia; instead of returning home to a successful career, he died of dysentery at the age of thirty-five.

Sometimes, of course, the artist just could not find the right sitter for the project he had in mind. This irritating setback happened to Zeuxis in Ancient Greece, when he was commissioned to paint a Venus. Having looked without success for a suitable candidate, he was in despair, so he sent for all the most beautiful girls in the town, and selected five. Then he painted the arms of one; the hair of another; and the eyes of a third. Apparently his theory was that a variety of pieces make up a good whole.

Poor old Zeuxis would have been off and running if he had had Lady Emma Hamilton as a model. This lady, as everyone knows, was Lord Nelson's mistress; she was also a woman who had played the field (before and during the time she was married to Hamilton), who liked to drink, and who danced on the tops of tables in a state of undress. All of which would make her either first or last on your party list, depending on your taste.

But she was certainly beautiful, and attracted many admirers, of which the besotted George Romney was one. Born in Lancashire, he lived there until he was twenty-eight when he left his wife and made a career in London, where he became infatuated with Emma Hamilton. In fact, he was so smitten that he couldn't paint her enough, and she turned up in numerous disguises as various mythological goddesses, her pretty face adorning many country houses to this day. Unfortunately, after Nelson died, she was shunned by society and finally expired, a penniless alcoholic, in France. Romney didn't do much better. In old age, he became senile and finally left London to return to his long-suffering wife, who nursed him until he died.

Reynolds also painted famous ladies of easy virtue, one of the most notorious being the Contessa della Rena. This woman became known as 'La Rena,' and was married to an Italian merchant who lived in Florence. Her 'hospitality' was well known to all the traveling Englishmen who visited her, her lovers including the Marquis of Marigny. Her life was easy and comfortable, but she still grew bored with Italy and returned to London in the dubious company of the Earl of Pembroke. Two years later, she became the mistress of the unsavory Earl of March, with whom she remained for eight years.

But her reign was over when March asked the dissolute George Selwyn to do his dirty work for him and explain to 'La Rena' that she was out and a child dancer was in. The news was not received with great delight, and soon after she got her marching orders, 'La Rena' moved back to Italy. Years later, the obnoxious Selwyn declined to visit her — because she had aged badly!

Reynolds also had the dubious pleasure of painting the second son of George II: William, Duke of Cumberland. He was an army officer whose brutal treatment of the Jacobites led to his nickname, 'The Butcher.' He looked the part, too. Blind in one eye and grossly overweight, he weighed 280 pounds, and although he hardly qualified as a pretty picture, many copies of his portraits were made for the officers who served with him.

Devoted as his crazed underlings might have

been, his father was immune to his attractions, and on one occasion the king greeted him with the immortal line 'Here is my son who has ruined me and disgraced himself.'

Raphael was possibly one of the few artists who was well enough known, and well enough liked, to have gotten away with realism in a portrait. This is not to be recommended otherwise, especially with the rich and influential, who were quick to take offense with lesser painters. Many artists have found themselves prematurely retired or banished because of an overrealistic portrait. But Raphael survived, painting the Vatican librarian, Signore Inghirami, complete with his squint, and Leo X like a lecherous Mr. Magoo.

We will never know for certain, but possibly Leo X *did* take his revenge, because later, when Raphael was hurriedly summoned to see the Pope, the artist arrived hot and sweating and had to cool his heels for hours, waiting in a freezing room. This sudden chilling led to pleurisy, and Raphael died a few days later.

Hogarth didn't have to cope with Popes, but due to the times in which he lived, this artist painted some sitters who were notorious even in those days — a feat that took some doing. Some were bawds or rakes; others were not as well known but displayed the manners and attitudes of the day. A good example of this is the middle-aged man in the painting *The Countess's Morning Levée*, who wears a fan on his wrist to indicate that he is a homosexual.

Frank Matthew Schutz was *not* a homosexual,

but he was a poor husband, and he had a wife whose patience was exhausted by his womanizing and drinking. In order to make her point, Mrs. Schutz commissioned Hogarth to paint her husband as *she* usually saw him. The result was an eye-opener. Romantic as Mr. Schutz may have appeared to his mistress, his wife had to put up with the morning fallout after a night of binging, and this was not a pretty sight. His portrait is probably the only painting of a man with a hangover being sick while clasping one fevered hand to his head, his lips no doubt forming the immortal words *Never again*.

Hogarth also painted Francis Dashwood, a creepy, sexually perverted man. His own peculiar passion was for sex that related to, and debased, Christianity, and in order to satisfy his urges, he founded a 'monastic' order that met in an abbey that Dashwood had decorated with deviate, erotic designs. His sexual leanings resulted in quite a following, and his love of dressing up in religious clothes apparently added spice to his sexual acts.

Dashwood was obviously one jump ahead of the butterfly nets, but he was also rich, and when he commissioned Hogarth to paint him 'at his devotions,' the artist was only too happy to oblige. In this painting, Dashwood is depicted as a devout believer, but instead of worshiping the crucifix, he is worshiping a nude woman, and his Bible is a novel of erotica. The picture pleased Dashwood enormously, but he soon tired of it and had himself painted again by Knapton, in the guise of St. Francis — a wise move, in a way, as he was the patron saint of animals.

Velázquez would not have liked Dashwood, although he did paint some unusual people, and needed all his skill as a portrait painter to make a reasonable picture out of the Duke of Olivares. This gentleman was the epitome of what used to be called a 'bounder.' He was the son of an ambassador, and although he had been marked out for a career in the Church, he changed direction when his brother died, and went into politics instead. His first political move was to marry the very homely Doña Iñes de Zuniga, who was transformed into a beauty when Olivares discovered that she was the lady-in-waiting to the Queen. By marrying her, he thought that he would be made into a grandee. He was wrong.

Stuck with a very unappetizing wife, Olivares plodded on and plotted for several years until he was finally invited to court — and outstayed his welcome when Philip IV made him prime minister, a post he retained for twenty-two years. Due to his power and wealth, he was soon impossible to control and much hated. With typical duplicity, Olivares crawled to the king and was brutal to the nobles, his mendacious, vicious, and disruptive temperament hinting at mental instability.

It was Coco Chanel who said that everyone deserves their face by the time they are forty. Well, going on a likeness of Olivares, and a contemporary description, he must have done some heinous things. 'His shoulders are so rounded that he has been described as a hunchback . . . [he has] a very pronounced chin . . . a large head that leans forwards, a vast forehead, yellowy skin, and a menacing and sly look in his eyes.'

Add to that the fact that he wore a wig that would have looked at home on a chorus member of *The Mikado*, and we have a very odd bird indeed. But, odd as he was, Olivares controlled the king until Philip IV finally abandoned him; humiliated in exile, he died insane soon after.

Regal portraits were always in demand when there were no newspapers, so royal painters such as Velázquez were kept very busy. He painted all the members of the royal family, the children who lived and those who died, and even their dogs, yet his art is cool and sometimes strangely concealing. From his paintings of the tragic Queen Isabella, it is difficult to remember that this woman gave birth to and buried four children, was repeatedly and viciously insulted by Olivares, was humiliated by her husband, Philip IV, and had to endure the shame of his many affairs, none of which he took the trouble to hide.

Even visiting ambassadors commented on the wretchedness of her life: 'The queen is much afflicted by the dissolute life led by her husband,' and again: 'The queen leads a very melancholy existence . . . more preoccupied with medicine bottles than with festivities.'

★ ★ ★

Kitty Fisher would never have put up with such treatment. As an infamous courtesan in the eighteenth century, she was a greedy, child-hating, manipulating call girl, who managed the incredible feat of astonishing Casanova by giving a new meaning to the term nouvelle cuisine when she ate a slice of bread with a twenty-pound note in it. (Remember how much that would be worth now, about one thousand pounds — all gone in one gulp.) Rumors abounded about her, and about the unpleasant means by which she aborted any unwelcome pregnancies. After all, being pregnant would have hindered her career. But looking at Reynolds's portrait of her, it is very difficult not to be attracted, and almost impossible to relate her appearance to her nature.

As an artist well used to playing tricks with a portrait, van Dyck would have recognized her type immediately. He was called in to paint the rich, powerful, and respectable — or those rich and powerful enough to pay to *look* respectable. A fine example of the latter can be seen in the portrait of Lady Digby as 'Prudence.' Well, she might have been prudent by name, but not by nature. In fact, she was sufficiently notorious in her youth to be called a 'Celebrated beautie and courtezane,' and was a long-term mistress to the third Earl of Dorset. But then she met and married Sir Digby (whose mother was not as enamoured with her as her son was) and apparently turned into a good and respectable wife. At least, that was the official version.

But people have long memories and, when Lady Digby died, van Dyck was called in to do a whitewash job and paint the two-day-old corpse in a manner that would serve as a suitable memorial. The result was a triumph of PR over fact — Lady Digby is depicted as 'Prudence,' in a white dress, with two white doves, looking like a magician's assistant. On top of this, various allegorical symbols cluster around her feet to show her triumph over the vices, while three bored-looking angels chorus overhead like a youthful version of the Beverley Sisters.

Still, at least van Dyck didn't have his reputation to worry about — which is more than can be said for Carreño de Miranda. This artist is not very well known, and no wonder, if his talent was constantly strained by sitters such as Eugenia Martinez Vallejo, 'La Monstrua.' This lady was not fat, she was *gigantic* — her broad face framed by hair decorated with ribbons the size of windmill sails, her dress hardly smaller than a wedding marquee, her tiny hands poking out of the voluminous sleeves like pink mice peeping from under a mass of bedclothes.

It is a strange fact, but many of the worthies of yesteryear were often clock-stoppingly plain. Just look at Monsieur de Norvins in the National Gallery, and you'll see what I mean. This gentleman, painted by Ingres, was the Chief of Police of the Roman State, and acts the part by staring out at the viewer and managing to evoke the same feeling that you get when there is a police car following you down the street. And why is his left hand tucked into his jacket? Did he have delusions of Napoleonic grandeur? Was he having a furtive scratch? Was he checking his heart rate? Or feeling for his wallet?

It is no wonder that some artists turn away from human sitters and look for inspiration elsewhere. Otto Marseus van Schrieck was a seventeenth-century Dutch painter who worked for the Grand Duke of Tuscany and became famous for his still lifes — all of which sounds pretty boring until you know the reason *why* he became so well known. The fact was that within every painting there were many individual portraits of insects — and not only insects either; there were snakes and lizards and every creeping thing that any creeping patron could desire. Schrieck grew so attached to his tiny sitters that he actually built up a museum for them, and fed them on the exotic plants he grew there, no doubt feeling that they had more than earned their keep.

Some other creatures did not fare so well. What happened to the dog in the far left-hand side of Velázquez's painting *Philip IV Hunting Wild Boar*? The poor animal is miles away from the boars (the four-legged ones, that is) and is surrounded by concerned onlookers. Must we presume that Philip IV was not only a plain, mean-minded man but that he was a bad shot as well? Or was it an example of a sitter who unfortunately met his end before the painting did?

But, forgetting animals for the minute, sometimes when an artist cannot afford a model, he has to make do with using family or friends. At other times, he becomes obsessed with one model, as did Andrea del Sarto, but generally an artist will try and change his sitters frequently for the sake of variety. This was not the case with Pietro Longhi, who not only used the same model three times but painted her three times in the same dress. Just look at the woman in the blue dress in the National Gallery, London, who appears in *Nobleman Kissing a Lady's Hand*, *Interior with Seated Woman and Man*, and then again in *Exhibition of a Rhinoceros*.

Do note, however, that in the last painting she is wearing a *mask*. Is this to prevent recognition? Or is she the first example of an artistic gate-crasher?

However they get into the paintings, some sitters have to endure very uncomfortable conditions for the sake of art. When Millais was painting the doomed Elizabeth Siddal, the lady had to languish for hours in a tub of lukewarm water, pretending that she was the drowning Ophelia. On many occasions, the water cooled off, and once, when Millais was driven by inspiration, he failed to notice that the candles underneath the bath (which warmed the water) had gone out. The temperature dropped rapidly and only Elizabeth's complaints saved her from the same fate as Ophelia.

Amusing as this sounds, Elizabeth Siddal was less than pleased and caught a severe chill after this episode. In fact, she was so annoyed that she threatened to sue Millais; however, the timely intervention of her husband, Rossetti, prevented another scandal.

Not all female sitters were as lovely as Elizabeth Siddal; some were not so much 'La Bella' as 'La Repella.' For example, there is *The*

Grotesque Old Woman painted after Quentin Massys, a lady more likely to raise the eyebrows than the pulse. And what about *The Two Tax Gatherers* in the National Gallery, London? The old woman is lined, wizened, and hunched over an account book, her male companion leering idiotically out of the painting, while both are dressed in fabulous, surreal costumes. Some of Brueghel's sitters weren't too pretty, either. In the *Adoration of the Kings*, his two kings kneeling in front of Christ are as weird as some of Hieronymus Bosch's characters, although they do have *all* their limbs, not like Jean Delville's *Orpheus*, which represented the head of his wife — nothing else, just the head.

In a very unfair battle of the sexes, female sitters nearly always come off worst, and even if they weren't being decapitated in paintings, they suffered in real life. Take Mrs. Kirke, for example. This lovely woman was painted by van Dyck, her portrait betraying nothing of her tragic death. She was dresser to Queen Henrietta and was married to the king's dresser, a man who also organized the masques and balls for the court, at which Mrs. Kirke performed. Unfortunately, for all her talent, she was not Esther Williams, and, when the queen's boat overturned after one masque, Mrs. Kirke drowned before anyone could save her.

Some other female sitters met *murderous* ends. Even though she was rich and powerful, Isabella de' Medici found that her enemies were closest to home. Her husband, having fallen in love with another woman, plotted to have her killed. The means he chose were particularly brutal. During a meal, he had a rope passed down by this accomplices from the room above, and then choked his wife, the rope being pulled back out of sight afterward.

Allori's *Judith with the Head of Holofernes* is justifiably well known. What is not so well known is that the sitter for Judith was the artist's mistress, Mazzafirra. In fact, the picture became quite a family affair — the old woman who plays the part of Judith's assistant is actually Mazzafirra's mother, and the amputated head, which is being held with such calm triumph, happens to be a portrait of Allori himself — after he had grown a beard to look the part!

By a strange coincidence, William Howard, Viscount Stafford, met his Maker with his head detached from his body. This feral-looking individual, who sat for van Dyck, was guilty of a variety of salacious vices, possessed a vile temper, and generally acted in a way that did nothing to add to his popularity at home or at court. In fact, it was said that he was 'not a man beloved, especially of his own family.'

No doubt they were thinking of getting him adopted when, as luck would have it, William was caught and beheaded for plotting against the king.

Certain deaths have a degree of dignity, a nobility that makes them even more poignant. Being shot is a macho way to go; being poisoned is commonplace; and being finished off in the middle of your ablutions is definitely bourgeois. David's painting of *Marat assassiné* depicts the victim as a stiff in a tub — a tub Marat worked in most of the day (because he had an unpleasant skin condition), while wearing a shower hat and writing his papers on the top of what appears to be an orange crate.

There is quite a tradition of the posthumous portrait. Indeed, in English art of the fifteenth century, it was commonplace for a painter to portray the husband and wife and their children — including the ones who had died. These dead children were painted suspended in midair, their bodies undergoing some kind of artistic levitation a couple of feet above the ground. Take a look at some of the early English paintings and you'll see dozens of floating infants — the principle being that they existed somewhere between heaven and earth.

There have been other posthumous sitters, and once Gainsborough was asked by a patron, General Sloper, for 'an interview between the late amiable Mrs. Sloper, who is to be *spiritualized*, and her two surviving daughters.'

But the most famous of all these posthumous portraits is probably that of Thomas Chatterton. In Georg Wallis's painting, *The Death of Chatterton*, the dead poet is draped over a mean little bed, his poems torn and scattered around him, his hair the color of a rusty gate, and his skin chalked up like Marcel Marceau. The picture suited the Victorian taste perfectly — here was the starving poet in the inevitable garret, having taken poison because he hadn't been an overnight success. (He was seventeen years old.) The subject obviously caught the

211

painter's imagination and Wallis was very faithful to the truth, actually visiting and painting the selfsame attic where the teenage Chatterton had ended it all.

There have been some *nearly* posthumous sitters, too. When Gainsborough was on holiday, a Mrs. Heathcote called on him and asked whether he would paint her last surviving son, as *she had lost five other children in an epidemic.* With true Christian charity, Gainsborough told her to clear off. Stung, Mrs. Heathcote then went away and came back the same afternoon with her son. The artist, by now embarrassed and more than a little ashamed, said, 'I will gladly comply with your wish.'

Esther Vanomrigh also employed the powers of persuasion, although in her case, they didn't work. The lovely portrait, by Millais, entitled *Vanessa,* depicts this lady, who had the misfortune to become obsessed with the novelist Jonathan Swift. Not that he didn't encourage her devotions. When he was in London, he called on her daily, encouraged her to study, and generally gave Esther the impression that life would be pretty dull without her. Alas, on leaving London for Dublin, his attitude changed, and while Swift found other diversions, Esther wrote letters to him, as many as four a week — delighting the Royal Mail, and infuriating Swift. Finally, he wrote back: Thanks, but no thanks.

But this was not to be the end of this sad tale. With the same stubbornness that affects all wronged women, Esther followed Swift to Ireland and tried to win him back; and with the same callousness that affects all arrogant men, Swift ignored her. As he lost interest, she lost face — and died embittered.

Other women learned how to use men. Courtesans such as Kitty Fisher made a career out of manipulation, but Elizabeth Gunning was just as deadly when she set her sights on someone. Having decided that she would marry the Duke of Hamilton, they were wed at midnight on St. Valentine's Day, using a bed-curtain ring to plight their troth (because her husband had gambled his money away). Elizabeth's notoriety was such that her appearance anywhere caused the same kind of commotion as Madonna's would now, and when the dissolute duke died, she wasted no time in getting remarried — choosing the Duke of Argyll this time.

Similar things were happening across the Channel. Manet's painting *Autumn* depicts Mary Laurent, an actress with a strong materialistic streak. She soon devised an alternative career for when she was out of work, and spent her spare time sleeping with a variety of powerful men. George Moore said of her, 'the daughter of a peasant, and the mistress of all the great men of that time.'

The acting profession as a whole is keen on making entrances, holding court, being the center of attention, and leaving a powerful impression. It was the same in the eighteenth century. In fact, when David Garrick was painted by Gainsborough, a contemporary related just how difficult a subject the actor was:

213

Sketching the eyebrows he [Gainsborough] thought he had hit upon the precise situation and then looked a second time . . . and found the eyebrows lifted up to the middle of the forehead . . . a third time they were dropped like a curtain, close over the eye.

Garrick had an infuriating personality, too, and when he was invited out to dine, he would arrive, talk loudly, give his opinion on everything, act out his current role, and then, just as everyone was finally getting their feet under the table, a minion would rush in, hotfoot, and say that Garrick was required elsewhere. There would be lots of apologies, extravagant gestures of regret, and a brilliant exit before the steam had died on the mock turtle soup.

Lady Castlemaine was no novice when it came to the dramatic gesture, either. The painting *Charles II and Lady Castlemaine* by William Powell Frith shows us a very autocratic lady, whose hand is being slobbered over by the king — an action remarkable in itself. The story was taken from Samuel Pepys's diary and demonstrates the power a woman can have over a man:

Though the king and my Lady Castlemaine are friends again she is not at Whitehall but at Sir Harvey's, whither the king goes to see her; but he says she made him ask for forgiveness on his knees, and promise to offend her no more . . . indeed, she hath nearly hectored him out of his wits.

Some sitters could have done with a good hectoring themselves. One of the most notorious sitters who came to pose for Thomas Lawrence was the frisky Princess Caroline — a lady who found herself repeatedly involved in self-inflicted scandals. Due to her visits to Lawrence, four witnesses testified that the princess had made herself 'familiar' to the artist, and although she was cleared of adultery, she was censured for her behavior toward Lawrence and for being 'incautiously witty' about her husband.

The case was notorious and helped Lawrence's career to no end, although Princess Caroline's regal progress was somewhat hampered, especially as she continued to behave most oddly in the years to come, appearing at a ball in Geneva bare-breasted and arriving at another reception with half a pumpkin on her head.

Even the mild John Constable was forced to refer to her as 'the royal strumpet . . . the rallying point for all evil-minded persons.'

But she did find much support elsewhere and, after the scandalous trial for divorce from her husband (the future King George IV), Caroline was vindicated when the bill was dropped. Yet if the people were on her side, she was far from being forgiven in royal circles, and when her husband entered Westminster Abbey for his coronation, she was refused admittance, even though she ran around hammering on each door and trying to get in. Three weeks later she was dead — not of a broken heart, as some claimed, but of a bowel complaint.

Rudeness to sitters wasn't unknown, either.

Rossetti often reduced Elizabeth Siddal to tears, and Gainsborough was frequently less than polite to his customers. The alderman Mr. Cunningham was one who felt the thick end of the painter's tongue when he arrived, duly dressed with a new five-guinea wig. Sitting down and arranging himself in the best light, he asked Gainsborough to take care to paint the dimple in his chin.

'Damn the dimple in your chin!' the artist replied shortly. 'I can neither paint that nor your chin, neither.'

That kind of remark generally results in lost sales, unless you are as well known and respected as Gainsborough. Holbein would have been very reckless to have tried out such tactics in the court of Henry VIII. In fact, very little is known of Holbein's life, but, having painted many important people who met with bad accidents, possibly he thought it was better to keep his head down rather than risk having it taken from him forcibly by an ax.

However, reserved as he was, Holbein did leave us a series of remarkable portraits of the important people of that time, although one of his most famous paintings, *The Ambassadors*, is not unique for the sitters you see but for the one you don't: What appears to be a very large, stainless-steel Frisbee in the foreground of the painting is actually a *skull*, belonging to the phantom third sitter. All you have to do to find him is to turn your head to one side, screw up your eyes, and there he is — the only deceased, distorted, deformed, and damn-near invisible sitter in the history of art.

216

10

What Artists Did to One Another

It seems reasonable that an artist should feel choked when a rival succeeds in getting the job he is after. It often means that the loser goes hungry for a while; any artist is entitled to feelings of boiling indignation. But murder? Even in the art world murder is excessive, and generally results in the termination of the murderer's career — which defeats the purpose entirely. Yet there always have been murders — for reasons of anger, jealousy, rivalry, or imagined slights. More often, there have been vicious attacks or fights among artists.

The comprehensive list of what artists have done to one another is so extensive that it would take another book to fully investigate every gory underhanded deed. Instead, for the present, let's look at a few examples to whet your appetite, and if you happen to be an art student, perhaps you can pick up a few tips.

Jealousy can sometimes be so potent that it achieves a form of immortality and exists after death. James Barry, the Irish painter, was encouraged by Reynolds in his youth. Later made a member of the RA (the Royal Academy having being formed by Reynolds), he was continually helped by the elderly, influential artist. Flattered by Dr. Johnson and supported by the powerful Edmund Burke, who were both friends of Reynolds, Barry progressed mightily, but as his fees swelled, as did his head, and soon he could hardly be persuaded to demean himself by painting portraits.

However, he was still elected as professor of painting at the Royal Academy, and his nastiness was humored until 1799, when he was finally *expelled* for his vicious, unprovoked attack on his peers, which he followed with a ferocious assault on the memory of the dead Reynolds. In a fine example of someone biting the hand that feeds them, Barry then demolished the wrist and most of the upper arm, his ingratitude repelling his patrons and his friends, who abandoned him to die in squalor.

At least Barry's descent was of his own making, whereas an outsider brought down poor Federico Barocci. This unfortunate man found that envy could be almost deadly in Renaissance Italy, and spent a great deal of his time looking over his shoulder. It is a splendid thing to be favored by Popes, as Barocci discovered when he worked for Pope Pius IV, but unfortunately it can also be dangerous. In Italy at that time, poisoning was an art form in itself, the initiated whipping up a terminal snifter with all the panache of a bartender mixing a good martini.

As frequently happened, Barocci's good fortune was resented, and while he was happily working in the Vatican, he was slipped a mickey by an envious rival who wanted to ensure that he wouldn't be too nifty with his brushes for a while. The while turned out to be four years.

Not everyone resorted to belladonna when more subtle means of attack were available. As we already know, Caravaggio was not a person who inspired warm feelings in others. In short, his temper made him feared, and his talent made his contemporaries envious. Giovanni Baglione — an artist of unremarkable and limited ability — worked hard without much acclaim until he became influenced by Caravaggio's paintings and was briefly inspired.

For a time, all went well, but Caravaggio liked insulting people the way that Mike Tyson likes thumping them, and before long he was making the kind of critical comments that usually lead to a few loose teeth.

But if Baglione was a quiet man, he was also a stubborn one, and, in an action that has secured his fame forever, he sued Caravaggio for libel (making his will at the same time, one imagines). Caravaggio did not like getting taken to court and, even though he won, he swore to get even. Baglione by this time had had enough of the lawsuit, the insults, and Caravaggio in particular, and determined to get *his* revenge. So he threw down his brushes and took up his pen. After working steadily for months, he completed the only contemporary biography of Michelangelo da Caravaggio.

Not an *i* was left undotted or a *t* uncrossed. In fact, although the book caused a violent rise in Caravaggio's blood pressure, it served two other purposes. First, it assured Baglione's revenge; and second, it pointed out his real talent as an investigative journalist. With enormous satisfaction, Baglione watched as the lurid exposé succeeded in ruining Caravaggio's reputation almost before the ink was dry on the page.

Vasari went into print, too, writing his famous book, *Lives of the Artists* which tells the stories of many of the most famous Italian painters. Michelangelo was 'divine'; Andrea del Verrocchio had 'a fine reputation'; and Raphael was treated to this rush of prose: ' . . . with wonderful indulgence and generosity heaven sometimes showers upon a person . . . all the favors and precious gifts . . . '

Vasari liked a florid style and he liked to flatter the artists — unless he took a dislike to them. And he *really* disliked Sodoma. After pages of gurgling eulogy of others, Vasari gives this unfortunate painter the kind of writeup normally confined to the pages of the tabloids, his fury and outrage scratching across the pages. It got so bad that if a story wasn't vile enough, Vasari would make something up in order to damn his victim even further.

Sodoma's response went along the immortal lines of 'Frankly, my dear, I don't give a damn,' and he proceeded to camp it up in a scandalous fashion, earning himself the nickname 'Il Mattaccio,' or 'The Arch Fool.'

But at least Vasari was open about his attack and didn't creep around trying to get his revenge in an underhand way. There is an unwritten law that says no artist can take rejection well — and that is an understatement. So it came to pass that Domenichino found that he had lost the commission for the San Andrea della Valle to his rival Lanfranco. Thwarted, he seethed with rage. In fact, he seethed for days and then decided that he was going to get his revenge.

So, in the dead of night, Domenichino crept into the chapel and unscrewed part of his rival's scaffolding, in the fervent desire that Lanfranco would soon be eyeball to eyeball with the God he was so busily painting. But it was to no avail; despite Domenichino's efforts, the scaffolding remained intact, and Lanfranco lived for another fifteen years before he could see whether his likeness was a good one.

Michelangelo inspired many a jealous feeling, too, and had suffered early on from having his nose smashed with a mallet, thus ensuring a Charlton Heston-type profile. Throughout his life, he was subject to attacks of bile. Indeed, the brilliant architect Bramante was so envious of Michelangelo that he managed to convince Pope Julius that the tomb Michelangelo was building for the Pope might be a bad omen. (I would have thought that any tomb was a bad omen; after all, you can't get unluckier than being dead.) Julius, duly terrified, abandoned the project and dismissed Michelangelo — without pay.

But jealousy has a way of rebounding, and Bramante's next little ploy was an immortal and everlasting failure. When the Pope was thinking of having the Sistine Chapel redecorated, Bramante spitefully suggested Michelangelo, thinking that, as he was a sculptor, he would make a sow's ear out of it, and thus ruin his reputation forever. The rest, as they say, is history.

The jolly little band of the Pre-Raphaelite Brotherhood wasn't immune to a bit of infighting either, especially when it came to a clash of personalities. Gabriel Dante Rossetti was what one might describe as an 'enthusiast,' and although his enthusiasm was appreciated in some quarters, it was not in others.

Ford Madox Brown, by contrast, was a nervous, easily irritated character, suspicious of everything that moved and of everyone who breathed. When he received a letter from the young Rossetti (who wanted to become his pupil) packed with the kind of voluminous praise at which Italians excel, Ford Madox Brown viewed the letter in a typically English way and took offense. He also took up a large walking stick with the express desire of rapping out an aria on Rossetti's head.

Luckily, the Italian managed to persuade his outraged visitor of his sincerity, and was duly employed as Madox Brown's apprentice. However, not all members of the PRB were such strong personalities; Holman Hunt was easily overawed by his loudmouthed peers, and was even heard to remark once, 'I feel frightened when I paint a flower.'

He wasn't the only member who was easily intimidated by the tougher artists. When John Millais painted daffodils in a picture together with roses, it was hardly a capital offense; it merely suggests that he was not an avid floral arranger. However, Rossetti, in true fashion, went ape and screamed abuse, insisting that both flowers could not bloom at the same time and that they be painted out of the picture. Instead of tipping half a can of turpentine over the demented Italian, a cowed Millais turned back to his canvas and obliterated the daffodils with all the savagery of a sudden frost.

It would seem that jealousy was not uncommon in English art. John Sell Cotman was a gifted artist in watercolor and oil and was a rival to John Crome, an artist who was working at the same time. Crome was a drinker and a businessman; Cotman was a bighead and a fool. Resenting Crome's good fortune, Cotman burned with envy and was delighted to receive the news that Crome had died and that his family was destitute.

With a remark that shows his character to its full advantage, he said: 'My oft-told dream terminated with the success of myself and my family, and the downfall of the family of Crome.'

But curses, like chickens, come home to roost, and Cotman's career ended in poverty and madness, his own children carrying his insanity into the next generation.

The law is always a good way to lose a reputation and a fortune. Even so, some people cannot resist the courts — and Whistler was one of them. James Abbott McNeill Whistler was an American who came to London to live and work. He was soon very successful, and enjoyed life as a dandy and lethal wit. Even Oscar Wilde, who had never been slow off the mark himself,

223

appreciated his snappy patter and, after one devastating riposte, turned to Whistler and commented, 'I wish I had said that.'

Without turning a hair, Whistler responded, 'You will, Oscar, you will.'

But Ruskin was not impressed with Whistler the man, or Whistler the artist, and after his painting *Nocturne in Black and Gold* was exhibited, Ruskin accused the artist of 'flinging a pot of paint in the public's face.'

Stung, Whistler sued him and took him to court, where many heated exchanges took place. On one occasion, Ruskin asked Whistler how he dared to ask so much for a painting, and Whistler replied, 'I don't ask it for a painting, but for the experience of a lifetime.'

In the end, Whistler won the case; but as he was awarded only a fraction of the damages, he spent the following years working to pay off his legal costs.

There is nothing quite like a witty riposte but, regrettably, Michelangelo never managed to deliver one. He could sculpt and paint like a god, but he opened his mouth only to change feet. According to Vasari: One day, in a vain attempt to undermine the elegant Raphael, who was parading around with his doting minions, Michelangelo called out, 'You walk with your court, like a prince.' To which Raphael replied, 'And you walk alone — like the hangman.' This was a merry little quip, which no doubt endeared him to Michelangelo even more.

But at least he was immune to jealousy, whereas Andrea del Castagno reveled in it. A gifted artist, he was also something of a thug and started his career by painting anarchists being hanged by their feet, thereafter earning the nickname 'Andreino degli Impiccati,' which means 'Andrea of the Hanged Men.'

With this charming sobriquet, Andrea left for Florence and flourished, just as his jealousy did, and before long he had come to hate his contemporary Domenico, who was working on a chapel fresco. Not that Andrea loathed him to the exclusion of all others; oh no — he would go around carping about everyone, criticizing their work and pointing out their artistic faux pas like a malicious Mr. Chips.

Meanwhile, Andrea's jealousy of Domenico smouldered on, the latter blissfully unaware of the situation. Being a bit thick, Domenico fell for Andrea's flattery and welcomed his companionship, spending far too much time with him. And while Andrea plotted, his supposed friendship with Domenico provided the perfect cover. But things came to a head after they finished their work on the chapel — and Domenico's artistry was praised to the skies.

His envy chewing pieces out of him, Andrea decided that Domenico must go. So one evening when Domenico went for a walk, Andrea declined to go with him and stayed in the studio. Domenico walked on, blithely unaware of any danger until he was struck from behind with a lead weight. After giving him a good working over and leaving him for dead, Andrea returned to the studio. One can only imagine his face when he was told the dreadful news by his

225

servants and ran out to find Domenico still alive. Cradling the dying man in his arms (and no doubt giving him the odd thump when no one was watching), Andrea wailed and lamented until, after an irritating delay, Domenico finally died.

The postscript to this is very interesting. No one realized what actually had happened, and Andrea went from strength to strength without the faintest suspicion attaching itself to him. The mystery was never solved until Andrea fell ill; on his deathbed, he finally confessed to killing Domenico, no doubt hoping for absolution. The priest absolved him but, with any luck, Domenico was already waiting at the Pearly Gates with his own piece of lead piping.

Other artists were prepared to wait for revenge instead of taking the drastic step of murder. The seventeenth-century Italian Barbieri was called Guercino ('squint-eyed') as a child and the nickname stuck. Yet his physical handicap doesn't seem to have held him back as much as other artists managed to. Guido Reni (the oldest virgin in Italy) despised him and accused Guercino of copying his work, stealing his ideas, and generally undermining him. With true paranoia, Reni went on so long and so alarmingly that Guercino moved out of Bologna and set up his own studio, out of town and out of earshot.

But with delicious irony, Reni died long before Guercino did. As soon as the latter heard the news, he rang Pickfords, packed up his tea chests, and moved back to Bologna to make a killing. Once there, he not only set up his own flourishing studio but, in a splendid act of revenge, he took on Reni's workshop as well, and cornered the artistic market for the next twenty-two years.

Professional attacks are one thing, but it is a brave man who gets involved in another's emotional affairs. Unfortunately, the love life of Andrea Mantegna proved too great a temptation for some. As a creative and intelligent painter (and playwright), Mantegna soon realized that the kind of lives his fellow artists lived were not for him. He disliked arguments and bad feeling and concentrated on his work instead — until Jacopo Bellini upset his routine.

Thinking that Mantegna looked like a good catch for his daughter, Bellini tried to persuade the reluctant artist to marry her, without realizing that a rival named Squarcione wanted the young woman for himself. When Squarcione heard the news, he swore revenge on Mantegna, hating him with the same depth of passion with which he loved Bellini's daughter.

Critical and spiteful, Squarcione tore Mantegna's work and personality to shreds, trying to belittle him and make him look foolish. Soon the whole town was talking about the feud, wondering what was going to happen and which man would marry Bellini's daughter. Finally, the patient Mantegna responded. Taking a revenge open only to artists, he hid himself away behind locked doors, working day and night. A week later, he invited the townspeople in to see his magnificent fresco on the chapel walls of St.

Christopher in Padua. They marveled, they wondered, then they laughed, because there, depicted as an 'ugly pot bellied figure' was Squarcione, immortalized forever on the chapel walls.

Having stressed humor throughout this book, it seems fitting that we should end not with a murder but with a ludicrous argument. And there was no one quite as ludicrous as Gustave Courbet at times. This was a man who made his feelings known on every subject in the universe — often unwisely.

Naturally, the critics loathed him, but his antics fascinated the people of France and, as he had a wonderful gift for self-publicity, he soon became well known. Regrettably, his notoriety galled other artists, especially the irritable Couture, who tried to humiliate Courbet by mocking his work and insulting him in public, calling him a variety of things — none of which was flattering.

But on one occasion, Couture's mouth ran away with him and a violent quarrel broke out in a restaurant; Couture insulted Courbet and then climbed onto a table to make his point from a more advantageous angle. Gustave Courbet followed suit, and because he was a huge man, he towered over the diminutive Courbet. By this time, people were peering in at the windows and doors to watch the ferocious argument. Such was the furor that even the artist Diaz, who had only one leg, tried to join the two shouting men on the table, but failed, his part of the argument continuing from floor level.

The upshot of the whole tirade was that Courbet and Couture calmed down and behaved like the two grown men they were, swearing never to speak to each other until the end of the century.

The fight took place in 1859.

Famous Last Words

Although many artists had a lot to say in their lifetimes, it would seem that the Grim Reaper rendered most of them speechless at the end. What follows are the only recorded instances of famous last words.

John Crome
'Hobemma, Hobemma, how I love thee.'

William Etty
'Wonderful! Wonderful, this death.'

Camille Pissarro
'Jesu!'

Thomas Gainsborough
'We are all going to Heaven, and van Dyck is of the company.'

Bibliography

Having done all my own detective work, and having gone to numerous exhibitions and given myself sore feet doing gallery marathons, I would still like to thank the following for their invaluable help.

CATALOGUES

Royal Academy of Arts: *Masters of 17th-century Dutch Genre.*
Royal Academy of Arts: *The Orientalists.*
Tate Gallery: *Joshua Reynolds*
Victoria and Albert Museum: *100 Great Paintings in the V&A.*

BOOKS

Blunt, Wilfred. *England's Michaelangelo: A Biography of George Frederic Watts.* London: Hamish Hamilton Ltd., 1978.
Boon, K. G. *Rembrandt: The Complete Etchings.* New York: H. N. Abrams, 1963.
Briou, Marcel. *The Medici.* London: Ferndale, 1980.
Christian, John. *Symbolists and Decadents.* New York: St. Martin's Press, 1978.
Daudy, Philippe. *The XVIIth Century.* London: Heron, 1968.
Descargues, Pierre. *Goya.* New York: Crescent Books, 1979.

Evans, Ivor, ed. *Brewer's Dictionary of Phrase and Fable*. Harper and Row, 1989.

Field, D. M. *The Nude in Art*. London: Hamlyn Publishing Group, 1979.

Flamand, Elie Charles. *The Renaissance*. London: Heron, 1968.

Galt, Giuseppe., ed. *Gainsborough*. New York: G. P. Putnam's Sons, 1969.

Guratzsch, Herwig. *Paintings of the Low Countries*. London: Jupiter Books Ltd., 1981.

Haak, Bob. *Rembrandt's Drawings*. Translated by Elizabeth Willems-Treeman. New York: The Overlook Press, 1976.

Harris, Nathaniel. *A Treasury of Impressionism*. New York: Crescent Books, 1979.

Hilton, Timothy. *The Pre-Raphaelites*. New York: Thames & Hudson, 1985.

Hirsch, Diana. *The World of Turner*. New York: Time-Life Books, 1969.

Hobson, Anthony. *J. W. Waterhouse*. Oxford: Phaidon, 1989.

Holst, Niels von. *Creators, Collectors and Connoisseurs: The Anatomy of Artistic Taste From Antiquity to the Present Day*. Translated by Brian Battershaw. New York: G. P. Putnam's Sons, 1967.

Jacobs, Michael, and Warner, Malcom. *Art and Artists in Great Britain*. Oxford: Phaidon, 1980.

Kitson, Michael. *The Complete Paintings of Caravaggio*. New York: H. N. Abrams, 1969.

Lennie, Campbell. *Landseer: The Victorian Paragon*. London: Hamish Hamilton Ltd., 1975.

Lindsay, Jack. *Courbet*. London: Jupiter Books Limited, 1977.

Links, J. G. *Canaletto*. Ithaca: Cornell University Press, 1982.

Lucie-Smith, Edward. *Symbolist Art*. New York: Thames & Hudson, 1985.

Marchiori, Giuseppe, ed. *Delacroix*. New York: G. P. Putnam's Sons, 1969.

Meehsam, Gerd, ed. *French Painters and Paintings from the Fourteenth Century to Post-Impressionism*. New York: Ungar Publishing Co., 1970.

Millar, Oliver. *Van Dyck in England*. London: National Portrait Gallery, 1982.

Milner, Frank. *The Pre-Raphaelites*. Liverpool: National Museums & Galleries on Meyerside, 1988.

Mills, John F. *Art Facts and Feats*. New York: Sterling Publishing Co., 1980.

Murray, Linda, and Murray, Peter. *The Penguin Dictionary of Art and Artists*. New York: Penguin, 1987.

Noakes, Aubrey. *William Frith: Extraordinary Victorian Painter*. London: Jupiter Books Ltd., 1978.

Osborne, Harold, ed. *The Oxford Companion to Art*. New York: Oxford University Press, Inc., 1970.

Plumb, J. H. *The Pelican Book of the Renaissance*. Middlesex: Penguin, 1982.

Potterton, Homan. *The National Gallery*. New York: Thames & Hudson, 1989.

Richardson, Joanna. *Gustave Dore: A Biography*. London: Cassell, 1980.

Rossi, Filippo. *The Uffizi and Pitti*. Translated by Richard Waterhouse. New York: H. N. Abrams, 1967.

Thomas, Denis. *Everyone's Book of the Impressionists*. London: Hamlyn Publishing Group, 1980.

Vasari, Giorgio. *Lives of the Artists*. Translated by George Bull. New York: Penguin, 1966.

Wallace, Robert. *The World of Bernini*. New York: Time-Life Books, 1970.

Webster, Mary. *Hogarth*. London: Studio Vista, 1979.

Williams, Jay. *The World of Titian*. New York: Time-Life Books, 1968.

Wright, Christopher. *The Art of the Forger*. New York: Dodd Mead, 1984.

Young, Eric. *Francisco Goya*. New York: St. Martin's Press, 1978.

We do hope that you have enjoyed reading
this large print book.

Did you know that all of our titles
are available for purchase?

We publish a wide range of high quality
large print books including:
Romances, Mysteries, Classics
General Fiction
Non Fiction and Westerns

Special interest titles available in
large print are:
The Little Oxford Dictionary
Music Book
Song Book
Hymn Book
Service Book

Also available from us courtesy of
Oxford University Press:
Young Readers' Dictionary
(large print edition)
Young Readers' Thesaurus
(large print edition)

For further information or a free
brochure, please contact us at:
Ulverscroft Large Print Books Ltd.,
The Green, Bradgate Road, Anstey,
Leicester, LE7 7FU, England.
Tel: (00 44) 0116 236 4325
Fax: (00 44) 0116 234 0205

MASK OF FORTUNE

Alexandra Connor

As a child, Zoe Mellor craved her mother's love, but her mother only had eyes for her first child, Victor — and died without revealing why she had directed such rancour at her daughter. Motherless at sixteen, Zoe spends her young days looking after her father and adored brothers in Lancashire. Here, she discovers she has a talent for painting and art appreciation — which the conniving Victor persuades her to put to nefarious use. Zoe's meteoric rise in the glamorous world of international art is mirrored by her success as a forger, which makes the family a fortune — but also engenders jealousy and greed. Now Zoe risks losing everything she has always worked for: her reputation, and the love and security she has found . . .

THE WITCH MARK

Alexandra Connor

Alison had been blessed by nature all her life — only I knew the other, darker side of her character. And only I knew the pain — the torment — of a jealousy that could never be assuaged. Throughout our childhood, she stood in golden light, centre stage, while I, blinking through heavy spectacles, looked on . . . As we grew to adulthood, it seemed that the path fate had charted for her was smooth and straight and clear. Gradually I resigned myself to staying in her shadow, playing out the role of second sister. I would have been content that way — if only she had not fallen in love with Mark Ward . . .

THE SOLDIER'S WOMAN

Alexandra Connor

In Oldham in Lancashire, Faith and her brother James are raised by an aunt following the untimely death of their parents. While James works in their grandparents' photographic studio, Faith befriends the characters in the rag trade. But a sordid encounter causes Faith to mistrust men. However, she finds love with the charismatic wanderer Samuel Granger. Then during the Great War, despite being posted 'missing, presumed dead', he returns to her and baby Milly seriously injured. Struggling financially, Faith takes in a lodger, a Frenchwoman — a war widow with a baby. The two women become close friends. Then tragedy strikes, and Faith realises her trust has been betrayed. She wants revenge and determinedly sets out to reclaim the greatest love of her life.